Picture
Framing

Picture Framing

Rosamund Wright-Smith

Orbis Publishing · London

Many people have helped in the preparation of this book and deserve my thanks. In particular, I am indebted to Paul Mitchell for his chapter on the history of frames, and to Alan Edwards for his excellent work in constructing many of the frames used in the projects and for the loan of his home and pictures. I am very grateful to Jonathan Savill of the Rowley Gallery, London, who gave freely of his time, premises and materials. Special thanks must go to Karl Barrie and Jan and Geoffrey Wansell who allowed us to photograph inside their homes, and also to Richard Salmon for the loan of his pictures. I am grateful, too, to Emma Wood for her editing and general guidance, to Patrick McLeavey for his work on the design, and to Peter Kibbles whose patience and friendly advice was greatly valued when preparing the photographs.

Half title page: *Dick Salmon,* 1978, a water-colour on paper by Patrick Procktor, in a simple brass frame.

Printed in Italy by IGDA, Novara

ISBN 0 85613 051 6

Contents

1 A basic polished wooden frame for an acrylic painting on canvas
2 A mount and a painted frame with glass for a water-colour
3 A block-mounted poster
4 A leather-covered frame with a strut back for a photograph
5 An antiqued frame for a repaired map
6 A mount with a title opening and a silvered frame for a cleaned engraving

7 A glass trap to display both sides of a script on vellum
8 A shadow box for a three-dimensional ceramic on a linen backing
9 A gilded frame for velvet-mounted miniatures
10 A restored antique frame for a surface-cleaned oil painting

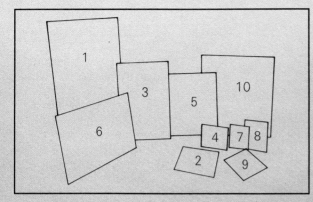

Pictured here are the finished frames from the ten different projects which are described in detail later in this book.

Why Frame?

More and more people are becoming interested in the idea of framing their own pictures. As the range of items to be framed grows wider all the time – from oils, water-colours and inexpensive reproductions, through photographs and other pictorial souvenirs, embroidery and collages, to signed limited editions by modern artists – so the price of professional framing seems to rise. At the same time, an abundance of craft shops and hardware stores selling a variety of do-it-yourself tools, has done much to encourage keen amateurs to attempt all sorts of handicrafts which were previously thought beyond their scope. Picture framing is one such craft.

Satisfying as it may be to select a style of frame which a professional will then make up, it is much more challenging – and ultimately rewarding – to choose the moulding, plan the decorative finish and make the frame with your own hands. Patience, precision and concentration, combined with the basic tools and materials, are all that is necessary to achieve perfectly acceptable results, and results that will improve with practice.

Not all pictures need conventional frames, of course, and throughout this book many and varied ways of displaying pieces of art will be suggested. Whatever the subject matter, however, it will not continue to look attractive or remain in good condition if simply hung and left without any regular care. The main reasons for using frames can, therefore, be summed up in just two words, pre-sentation and preservation.

Frames can be simple or elaborate, whichever is appropriate for the individual picture. The frame must complement the picture, not overpower it, and a rich mount (mat) and frame on a subtle painting can draw the attention away from the very object that it is meant to enhance. Different types of pictures demand different types of frames. Old water-colours, etchings or engravings, for instance, respond well to a combination of a card mount (either plain or with a line and wash treatment – see Project 2) and a plain wooden, natural or stained frame with a soft waxed finish. A gilt slip (liner) added between the mount and the frame is some-times an improvement. A traditional oil painting subject, say a portrait or landscape, can be greatly enhanced by a rich wooden, silver or gilt frame. Many such traditional frames can be obtained second-hand and refurbished.

In contrast, a modern painting or drawing very often needs no more than a wooden 'baguette' (un-rebated wooden moulding) or a simple metal frame around it. Tapestries and other wall hangings look attractive if hung with plain wooden polished rollers attached at top and bottom, or if they have a fabric mount of an appropriate texture and a frame. Collections such as medals or miniature paintings

Left: Various small pictures grouped with other small decorative objects around the fireplace of a traditionally furnished room include two water-colours, an etching, a silk embroidery and two gilt framed miniatures.

can be seen to advantage if mounted together on a fabric background such as linen, with the glass raised above them to form a shadow box effect (see Project 8), or set into velvet (see Project 9).

Works with a paper base, such as pen or pencil drawings, pastels, water-colours, etchings and lithographs, need glass and good backing to protect them from the ordinary household atmospheric conditions of heat, dust, smoke, grime and insects. Pictures hanging in steamy places such as kitchens or bathrooms should certainly be glazed, although an alternative is to glue them down and spray them with a protective lacquer as described in Project 3. Prints and photographs can also be block-mounted with bevelled edges and heat-sealed professionally.

When print reproductions, pictorial mementos or tapestries, for example, are just 'tacked' to the wall, they also gather dust and other marks. Ideally, all such works need preserving behind glass but not all require frames. One fairly cheap and quite effective idea is to enclose the picture under glass, backed by hardboard (masonite) and fastened with clips. This is especially useful for modern lithographs or silk-screen prints that have their own surrounds and do not therefore need mounts.

Oil paintings are not generally glazed (except in public galleries for security) as glass prevents the painting from 'breathing', but they are protected by a film of varnish or wax. The accumulation of grime on the surface of an oil painting takes years and, as it is so gradual, can go unnoticed by the owner so that subtle details of a painting are often lost under the dirt. Oils should therefore have their protective coating of varnish or wax removed and re-applied every few years. This is a job for the professional restorer, although anyone can achieve quite surpris-ingly good results from a simple, careful surface clean (see Project 10).

The personal taste of the owner and the surround-ings in which the work is to hang obviously influence the choice of framing. However, it is often hard to envisage the finished effect of a certain kind of mount and frame until they are actually assembled and fitted onto the picture. Throughout this book, therefore, we indicate how different colours and tones in mounts and frames influence the pictures around which they are placed.

Other factors to consider are placement and spacing on walls in relation to the size of room and picture, the important role of light, and the general design of the room. In the main, such details are finalized after the initial work of framing, but they are best borne in mind right from the start if the display of pictures is to be successful.

When hanging pictures, remember that all pic-tures, but especially oil paintings of value, should not be hung over or near heaters of any kind, as the rising hot air can damage the surface. Likewise, pictures hung in direct sunlight (particularly those with a paper base) will, in time, turn brown and water-colours may fade. I have seen a line and wash treatment on the mount of a water-colour faded out completely, although the painting itself was luckily unaffected. Remember that glass magnifies heat,

Why frame?

thus hastening such deterioration. This is the reason why art shops facing direct sunlight often have their windows coated with a thin, slightly coloured film which prevents the damaging rays of the sun from striking the pictures on display.

Indoor lighting varies greatly, whether natural or artificial, but is largely responsible for successful picture hanging. Individual picture-lights are sometimes used for older pictures with darker tones where the details are hard to discern, or where the pictures are out of range of other lighting. However, picture-lights are only really satisfactory if they are the right type and size for each picture.

Pictures should be hung within a reasonable distance of average eye-level, using about 1.5 m (5 ft) from the floor as an approximate guide. If there are more than one or two pictures to each wall, group them together in various ways, preferably not aligned in regimental fashion on one particular level, although a deliberately uneven arrangement can

look equally unnatural. Do not place two extremes of size together as the smaller will obviously be dwarfed by the larger. Indeed, a large, dominant picture or hanging may well demand a wall to itself. Smaller and medium sizes can, however, be arranged to form a pleasant group, even taking up virtually a whole wall.

Hints on general picture hanging and display will be found throughout the book, especially in relation to the particular projects. Ranging from a basic frame to a complicated piece of restoration, each project is complete in itself, but does assume certain knowledge to have been gained from the opening chapters. The techniques for different ways of mounting and framing ten disparate objects are fully described and then illustrated, step by step, in explanatory line drawings. It is very important to study the text at the same time as you follow the diagrams, in order to make the most effective use of this book.

Left: Three contemporary pictures in simple surrounds complement each other in both colouring and type:(far left) America, America or Sad-eyed Lady of the Lowlands, 1972, oil on board by Terry Ilott, has a flat steel frame made by the artist; side screws join it to the picture. (right above) Night and Day, 1973, by Robert Schmid, is in fact deceptively simple. It is oil on perspex, cut out and mounted on perspex and then framed in perspex layers by the artist. (right below) Abstract Composition, 1972, by

Rod Campbell, in water-colour, ink and pencil on paper is set in a plain grey mount with a flat black lacquer frame.

Below: A modern room setting, cool and casual, is dominated by the silk-screen print Twiggy by S. Colby, which has a plain aluminium foil-on-wood frame harmonizing with the chrome shelving unit and the frame of the chair. The clean, sharp lines of the plate glass shelves and the glass on the picture add precision to the overall effect.

The Framing Tradition
by Paul Mitchell

It is only in recent years that picture frames have become recognized as an art form in themselves. This subject is perhaps the least researched of any branch of art history, falling between the Fine Arts – painting, sculpture and architecture – and the Decorative Arts – furniture, objets d'art and crafts. Yet at different periods and to some degree picture frames have embodied all the principal fields of art. The finest frames were designed by artists and architects, and carved by sculptors. For centuries frames have been regarded as merely decorative accessories to paintings, vulnerable to change according to prevailing tastes and owners' surroundings. The concept that frames were often designed for specific pictures to form a stylistic unity has been so long overlooked that very few paintings have survived with their original frames. (This, of course, makes a study of the subject so elusive. Even in major museums paintings with original frames can often be numbered on two hands, if not one.)

There is, however, plenty of evidence to show that artists, together with their patrons, paid great attention to the framing of commissioned work. Numerous drawings of detailed frame designs survive, and occasionally frames designed in collaboration with artists were signed by the carver. For example, the magnificent frame in Giovanni Bellini's triptych in the church of Santa Maria Gloriosa dei Frari in Venice is signed and dated 1488 by the carver Jacopo da Faenza. Other forms of documentation are letters describing contracts, payments, and guild regulations. We know, for example, that Filippino Lippi received 200 gold escudos for painting the high altar in the Santissima Annunziata in Florence: the frame-maker Baccio d'Agnola, however, was paid 250 escudos and a further 200 were spent on the gilding. There is no doubt that the finest paintings stimulated a competitive response from their framers. Thus deeper understanding of a painting in its contemporary frame must follow from an investigation of the delicate and subtle interrelation with the frame itself.

The frame in its simplest form of a painted decorative border is recorded in ancient Egypt, Greece, Rome and in Carolingian art on wall paintings, mosaics and as linear relief sculpture. However, it was not until the emergence of the panel painting in the later Middle Ages that the frame truly became an independent art form. Free standing and movable panel painting appeared in the thirteenth century as part of the furnishings of medieval cathedrals and churches in Europe. They stood before or on altars and fulfilled a focal part of the church's liturgical and theological programme.

The earliest frames were literally part of the painting itself – being the raised edges of a panel remaining after the flat picture surface had been gouged out. The profile was often carved to imitate the stone architectural mouldings in the church. Generally the entire panel was gessoed and gilded with a punched and incised pattern marking the frame from the picture surface. This form of 'engaged' frame, as it is known, appeared on both church and private devotional panels throughout Europe. An early example, the *Wilton Diptych*, *c*.1395, is of French origin, while some of the richest surviving panels come from the Siennese school of the fourteenth century.

The vast cathedrals and churches built in Europe during the fourteenth and fifteenth centuries demanded far larger and more elaborate altarpieces. By bonding separate wooden borders to the edges of panels it became possible to construct large, independent multi-panelled pictures. Design was very clearly united to the church itself, the triptych forming a cross-section of the Gothic church where the higher central panel, the nave, is flanked by the aisle side panels. Components were the same as the architectural motifs: columns with tall finials separated panels, forming ribbed vaults terminating in the triangular roof section. This arrangement also echoes the images in stained glass between the columns and buttresses. Altarpiece frames demonstrate the harmony between sculpture and architecture in the great Gothic churches. They were designed and carved by the same teams of sculptors and masons who executed choir stalls, pulpits and screens. Some of the most elaborate examples are found in Northern Europe. They were intricate structures often with two sets of movable wings, such as the Altar of St Clare in Cologne. Unfortunately few survive in their original state. Two fine exceptions are *The Coronation of the Virgin*, 1394, (Metropolitan Museum of Art, New York) and Gentile da Fabriano's *Adoration of the Magi*, 1423, (plate I).

During the fifteenth century small panel paintings were more common in Northern Europe than in Italy and the earlier practice of making the panel and frame either from the same piece of wood, or from separate members – though conceiving it as a whole – continued. Whereas Italian frames carried medallions, Flemish portrait artists often painted inscriptions about the sitter along the sides of the frame. In the Netherlands frames sometimes took the form of a window opening, painted to simulate marble or stone through which the subject was viewed, such as Jan van Eyck's portrait of *Margaret van Eyck*, 1439, (Groenige Museum, Bruges). Occasionally this *trompe l'oeil* was carried further when hands or drapery were painted on the 'window ledge' of the frame itself, thus making frame and subject inseparable.

Plate 1 Gentile da Fabriano *Adoration of the Magi*, 1423, 302 × 282 cm (119 × 111 in), Uffizi Gallery, Florence

This is an advanced form of the Tuscan altarpiece composed of bold architectural elements having a more decorative than structural purpose. The angled projecting columns with lancet windows are linked by three Florentine arches carrying trefoils with pinnacles and painted medallions, embellished with ornate leafwork. The main components form a stage for the panoramic painting rather than being an independent structure as in earlier altarpieces.

Plate 2 Michelangelo Buonarroti *The Holy Family*,
1504, diameter 120 cm (47¼ in), Uffizi Gallery,
Florence

*There could be few better examples of the degree of
skill reached in Italian frame-making than this
exuberant work by the Siennese carver Antonio
Barile, especially commissioned for Michelangelo's
tondo. Antique geometric motifs of bead-and-reel
on the inner edge and egg-and-dart on outer are
contrasted by a complex organic pattern of tendrils,
grotesques and birds, derived from antique
arabesque ornament. This band is punctuated by
five heads on medallions whose positions are
related to and reinforce the composition of the
painting.*

The later fifteenth and the sixteenth century in Italy was a dramatic, exciting and highly significant era in the history of European art. Italian Renaissance, Mannerist and early Baroque picture frames are witness to this immensely creative period and the forms that developed there were adopted throughout Europe. Ecclesiastical and secular patronage of the arts has never been greater. Powerful merchants and nobles such as the Gonzaga in Mantia, the Medici in Florence, the Montefeltro in Urbino, as well as the great families in Venice and Lombardy, commissioned paintings covering a wide range of subject matter. The growth of secular painting and the novel surrounds of contemporary architecture generated many new styles of frame, with an unprecedented attention to their construction and decoration. New tools and practices developed and the most important artists supervised their own frame-making. Sketches and documents directly connect Botticelli, Fra Filippino Lippi, Michelangelo and Raphael with the framing of their paintings. Indeed, Botticelli re-introduced a new form of frame, the Tondo, based on the round terracotta medallions of Luca della Robbia. Perhaps the most elaborate surviving example surrounds Michelangelo's *Holy Family* (plate 2), executed by the Siennese carver, Antonio Barile.

Interest in the architecture and ornament of antiquity provided not only a new vocabulary of ornament but also novel methods of presentation, notably the so-called 'Tabernacle' frames. These took the classical form of a window with pilasters and entablature and were commonly used in Florence and Venice for both secular and devotional pictures. Filippino Lippi's *Madonna and Child with Saints and Donors* in Santo Spirito, Florence, is in such a frame. An outstanding example of the larger form of the design, known as the 'Aedicula' surrounds Giovanni Bellini's triptych in Venice, carved by Jacopo da Faenza in 1488. Its importance is twofold: firstly, the use of a classical base supporting two pairs of pilasters and entablatures linked by a central rounded arch, all covered in arabesque relief ornament; and, secondly, an illusory painted extension of the framework suggests that the figures appear as sculptures standing in niches. The picture frame has assumed the role of a three-dimensional stage.

Reflecting the linear quality of Florentine architecture and painting during the Renaissance, a straight moulded 'border' frame emerged. The basic form consists of a raised inner moulding separated from a higher, outer one by a wide, flat ornamental panel. The inner and outer edges are plain or carved with husks, ribbons or leaves, and act as inner and outer frames, with the panels as breathing spaces between the picture and wall surface. Methods of decorating the panels, which were similar to those of furniture and wall hangings of the period, saw many regional variations. Florentine, Bolognese, Neapolitan and Venetian frames all had their distinguishing features during the fifteenth and sixteenth centuries.

It was from these Italian forms that the French frame-makers of the sixteenth and seventeenth centuries drew much of their inspiration. Indeed, François I invited numerous Italian artists and craftsmen to France, notably Rosso and Primaticcio to supervise the Royal workshops at Fontainebleau for the interior decoration of the palace. By the end of Louis XIV's reign France had superseded Italy as the centre of European art. The growing size and importance of the middle classes in Northern Europe had created an enormous demand for lavish interiors and comfortable furnishings. Furniture making became a major industry and picture frames were one of the many products of vast centralized furnishing workshops. Previously designed by artists and sculptors, frames were now the responsibility of furniture designers and became an integral part of an overall decorative scheme. Louis XIV and his minister Colbert had founded the Royal Academy of Painting and Sculpture in 1663, bringing all the arts under crown supervision. The Academy's first president, the painter Charles Le Brun, co-ordinated the making of frames which were largely creations of the great ornamental designers Jean Le Pautre, Robert de Cotte, Jean Bérain and Daniel Marot. Their task was streamlined by the new, highly organized Paris guilds whose standards and practices were strictly controlled. Picture and mirror frames were made by the guild of cabinet-makers from designs by leading artists.

Against this background it becomes clear why the main types of French frames can be so readily identifiable compared to the complex regional styles in Italy. The typical Louis XIII frame is related to Bolognese and Venetian models in the use of overall shallow relief carving of oak or vine leaves and flowers. The silhouette is straight, having no projections, and the section is usually a flattened cushion or ogee. The principal innovation in the Louis XIV design is that the linear profile breaks out at the corners and centres. These are now focal points along the frame suggesting optically diagonal, horizontal and vertical links between opposite corners and centres. In seeking a reason for this change it appears that this profile offers both a reinforcement and stability to the strongly three-dimensional quality in Baroque painting. Fine examples are to be found in Nicolas Poussin's *The Rape of the Sabines*, (Metropolitan Museum of Art, New York) and his *Adoration of the Golden Calf* (plate 3). Seen in isolation these magnificent frames are dazzling, but it must be remembered that they were once part of an overall scheme in richly decorated French palace interiors. Paintings in such luxurious surroundings demanded frames of exaggerated opulence if they were not to look insignificant.

During the Régence period which followed, the Louis XIV design was modified by the elimination of ornament, leaving panels between the carved corners and centres, whose smooth profile was linked by a straight outer rail. It was from carving these intermediate panels that the characteristic Rococo form arose. French influence in the decorative arts was such that both Louis XIII and XIV frames were copied, with slight variations, in other European countries, principally England and the Netherlands.

Plate 3 Nicolas Poussin *Adoration of the Golden Calf, c. 1635–7, 154.3 × 214 cm (60¾ × 84¼ in),* National Gallery, London

Richness of ornament together with brilliant execution are the hallmarks of French frame-making. This late Louis XIV frame, c. 1715, is a masterpiece of French furniture in its own right and demonstrates that an important painting, especially by a native artist, stimulated the creation of an exceptional presentation.

Of particular note is the clear definition of ornament achieved by the technique of re-cutting perfected in France. The entire frame is carved in oak, several coats of gesso applied, followed by specialist 'repareurs' who recarved the forms with fine lines, sharpening edges and etching criss-cross patterns into the flat background areas.

Peace and prosperity in Holland during the seventeenth century led to the growth of an affluent class of shippers, merchants and bankers who gave wide patronage to the arts. This brilliant 'Golden Age of Dutch Painting' was naturally reflected in frame-making. The severe character of Dutch interiors and Protestant disdain for the opulence of gilding influenced the evolution of dark wooden frames with rippled border patterns. The ungilded frames which appeared in the sixteenth century as an interpretation of the Italian border frame, developed in a luxurious manner in the seventeenth century, with veneers in exotic woods and tortoise-shell. Holland's extensive international trade enabled the import of many varieties of ebony and other well-figured woods which determined the character and colour of frames and furniture in the Low Countries. As in France, the guilds of cabinet-makers were responsible for frame design and manufacture. A new ornamental 'language' evolved with a wide vocabulary of linear geometric patterns. Special milling machines were fitted with jigs and tools that could cut ripples, wavebands and basket weaves mechanically into ebony or fruitwood capping-strips and veneers. These were applied to the laminated frame carcase whose profile consisted of both flat surfaces and convex, concave or ogee curves. The immense variations made possible by this process are well demonstrated in the Rijksmuseum in Amsterdam and in the Mauritshius in The Hague, where more paintings in their original frames may been seen than anywhere else in the world. Jan Vermeer's *The Letter* (plate 4) is a typical example.

As the desire arose for greater ostentation in Dutch interiors, carved giltwood frames appeared. The most conspicuous was the so-called 'lutma' frame (named after the goldsmith John Lutma), whose style was derived from the sinuous, swirling

Plate 4 Jan Vermeer *The Letter, c.* 1660,
44 × 38.5 cm (17½ × 15¼ in), Rijksmuseum,
Amsterdam

*This characteristic seventeenth-century Dutch
frame in ebony with rippled mouldings is a total
contrast to its French counterpart in carved
giltwood. The frequent use of a 'bolection' shape
pushing the picture plane forward, and enormous
width of the frame in relation to picture size created
an optical isolation in cabinet-sized pictures that
was completely original. Within the vast, black
boundary of frame a picture's natural luminosity
is seen to its greatest advantage.*

Plate 5 Nicolas Lancret *The Music Lesson,* 1743,
89 × 90 cm (35 × 35½ in), Musée du Louvre, Paris

*This magnificent frame, one of a pair commissioned
for the Versailles apartment of the Duchess of
Châteauroux, epitomizes Rococo decoration in its
maturest form. Devoid of straight lines, the
asymmetrical profile and indented picture space are
striking in their freedom and informality. The
characteristic Rococo shellwork known as*
rocaille, *combined with C- and S-scrolls, carefully
echoes and unites Lancret's fanciful and
capricious scene.*

forms of Venetian and Florentine Mannerist ornament. The section was wide and flat, carved in high relief with undulating scrolls interspersed with flowers, fruit, branches, birds, emblems, shells and sea monsters. A fine example surrounds Jan Steen's *Feast of Saint Nicolas*, *c.* 1660 (Rijksmuseum, Amsterdam).

The arts in seventeenth-century England were influenced by either Holland or France; taste fluctuated with the political climate. Appropriately popular during the Commonwealth were the sober black Dutch frames in plain wood or with border mouldings, while French designs predominated after the Restoration in 1660, indicating the return to greater luxury. The important collection of painting formed by Charles I had stimulated frame-making, and guilds of joiners, carvers and gilders were established during his reign. The standard of craftsmanship received another boost towards the end of the century when thousands of talented Huguenot carvers, gilders and cabinet-makers fled France. The French patterns they brought with them eventually became widespread, though the accession of William and Mary to the English throne caused Dutch influences to be strengthened once again; Europe's most brilliant Baroque woodcarver, the Dutchman Grinling Gibbons, came to England, becoming master carver to George I in 1714. His carving of garlands, fruit, flowers, shells and heads was unsurpassed and has remained a constant source of inspiration for English carvers.

Political stability and prosperity in Europe during the eighteenth century opened new avenues in the decorative arts, dominated by the Rococo style. Originating in the interior decoration of Paris in the 1720s, it was essentially luxurious, frivolous, sensuous and aristocratic, a reaction against the weight of Baroque forms. Designers and carvers knew no boundaries and for the first time classical proportions were discarded in favour of what Hogarth defined as the 'serpentine line'. The frame, in every sense of the work, became a dominant feature in paintings, mirrors, and indeed enclosed and decorated virtually any flat surface. Ornament in the form of 'C' scrolls developed from Baroque strapwork and arabesque; foliage, palms, rushes, roses and shells were combined in freely flowing organic forms. Nicolas Lancret's *The Music Lesson* (plate 5) is a distinguished example of Rococo exuberance.

The principal exponent of this style in England was Thomas Chippendale, whose designs for furniture, including mirrors and picture frames, became widely circulated with the publication in 1754 of his pattern book *The Gentleman's and Cabinet-Maker's Director*. A magnificent expression of the Rococo idiom is Chippendale's frame for the portrait of the Prince of Wales, 1755 (Victoria and Albert Museum, London).

Inevitably Rococo frivolity could not endure and a sobering reaction came with the renewal of interest in antiquity. The Neo-classical movement, which began with the dramatic discovery of the buried cities of Herculaneum and Pompeii, found its purest expression in French picture and print frames during the last quarter of the century. The new vocabulary of classical ornament, namely pearls, acanthus, leaves, egg-and-dart, ribbon-and-stick, flutes and guilloche bands, was used as a linear decoration for frames. Dumont's oval frame (plate 6) illustrates how the typically austere, thin frame section was often harmoniously balanced by a Rococo wreath of leaves and flowers.

During the Napoleonic and Second Empire periods French frames were notable for their finely moulded decoration and unprecedented uniformity. Indeed, Napoleon had most of the Louvre's collection reframed in a manner appropriate to current themes of classical history paintings favoured by the Academy. No doubt encouraged by persuasive salesmen and the availability of frames, many other European museums and private collectors favoured a regimental reframing of paintings with the idea that overall uniformity was more important than careful, individual presentation. The loss of many original frames through such insensitive reframing programmes is utterly lamentable.

English Neo-classical forms are seen in furniture by Sheraton, Hepplewhite and the Adam brothers. Although the majority of academic Neo-classical frames imitated French Louis XVI examples, the frame most widely produced in England was the so-called 'Maratta' pattern, which was based on the late seventeenth-century Roman design attributed to Carlo Maratta. The hollow section or slight edge consists of a richly carved running leaf-and-tongue ornament, bordered by pearls and ribbons. A fine early variation, with carved gadroon ring on the top rail surrounds Gainsborough's portrait of *Mrs Siddons*, *c.* 1758, (National Gallery, London).

The Maratta frame continued to be popular well into the early nineteenth century when the mass production of picture frames began, facilitated by a new technology of applying moulded plaster ornaments to wooden profiles. Highly detailed relief patterns were carved into boxwood blocks, from which press mouldings were made in a plaster composition and sometimes with papier mâché. The vast output of paintings of all genres in Victorian England and elsewhere in Europe demanded a substantial frame-making industry which produced endless 'historical' styles. Variations of French Baroque, Rococo and Neo-classical designs proliferated. Reluctant to create a completely new style the frame-makers freely imitated and adapted earlier models and, using plaster, they produced them in a fraction of the time. John Constable's *The Haywain*, 1821 (plate 7), for instance, is in an intricate nineteenth-century plaster frame based on a French Régence pattern.

America, meanwhile, had been forming her own framing traditions. Initially artists and craftsmen followed Dutch and English examples, but when demand for carved and gilded frames outstripped supply, they devised mouldings which reflected local taste and materials. Most eighteenth- and early nineteenth-century frames were consequently made of ungilded wood; their straightforward quality echoed the prevailing styles of painting. The variety

Plate 6 Artist unknown *Portrait of a Lady,*
c. 1780, frame 106.7 × 80 cm (42 × 31½ in),
Waddesdon Manor, Aylesbury

This virtuoso frame, bearing the rare distinction of
the canvas signature of its maker T. Dumont, shows
the pureness and symmetry of the Neo-classical
style, crowned by the festivity of Rococo. The
brilliantly naturalistic wreath is a carving cadenza
following the disciplined slow movement of
classical ornament. Precision and sharpness rival
the ormolu castings on furniture.

Plate 7 John Constable *The Haywain*, 1821, 130.2 × 185.4 cm (51¼ × 73 in), National Gallery, London

The finest nineteenth-century landscape paintings are often seen to best effect in ornamental gilt frames of French origin. This mid-Victorian frame with applied plaster ornamentation is based on a French Régence pattern with an added glazing inlay. However, by comparison with the prototypes carved in oak, such decoration was not only over-intricate and unnaturally harsh in appearance but subject to relatively rapid shrinkage and deterioration.

of timber available in America enabled frame-makers to exploit the natural effects of wood finishes, often achieving a closer tonal harmony between painting and frame than their European contemporaries could with heavily gilded plaster frames.

The major European artistic movements from the mid-nineteenth century to the present day have yielded countless highly original framing solutions. The stereotype academic, historical frame gave way to highly individual frames designed by artists for their own pictures with little or no compromise to the demands of patrons or external surroundings. The painting and its frame were often conceived as one inseparable unit in a way that had not been entirely permissible since Gothic and Renaissance altarpieces.

This revolutionary freedom was exalted with pride by one of the founders of the Pre-Raphaelite movement, John Everett Millais. In 1851 he wrote about his frame for *Convent Thoughts* (Ashmolean Museum, Oxford): 'I have designed a frame for Charles' painting of lilies which I expect will be acknowledged to be the best frame in England.' Consisting of a flat surface with arched top and lilies in high relief along the upright sides, it is a unique combination of simplicity and ornament, of abstract geometry with organic form.

The authority of traditional brightly gilded frames was also rejected by the Impressionists and Post-impressionists. In order to isolate their delicate compositions of light and colour, they began to use plain mouldings, often with a flat section painted white or off-white instead. Although this may have been a technically correct solution, it was found inadequate by collectors, and today we are used to seeing the work of the Impressionists and their followers in beautiful, faded antique frames, occasionally early Italian, but more usually French seventeenth- or eighteenth-century frames such as that on Camille Pissarro's *Sunset at Eragny*, 1888 (Ashmolean Museum, Oxford). That these frames are successful is due to their balanced proportions and very subdued patina, and also because the scale of the carved ornament is generally in accord with the size of the brushstrokes of the painting.

In the 1880s George Seurat developed another entirely new approach to framing. He defined the

Plate 8 Georges Seurat *View of Crotoy, Amont,* 1889, 69.2 × 87.2 cm (27½ × 34⅛ in), Detroit Institute of Arts

The highly sensitive discipline of Seurat's pointillist technique meant that his compositions could not withstand being adjacent to a traditional frame. He devised an optical isolation by painting his own complementary borders, either on a flat frame or in this case on the canvas, which as he wrote in 1890, was '. . . in the harmony opposed to those of the tones, colours and lines of the picture'.

boundaries of many of his canvases with a border painted in the same pointillist technique as the composition, such as that on *View of Crotoy,* 1889 (plate 8). A key exponent of the Art Nouveau style, Henry van de Velde, carried this idea further in *A Garden in Calmpthout,* 1890, (Bavarian State Museum, Munich). Here the wide inner flat section, enclosed by a reeded moulding, is painted in a pointillist style vibrating in sympathy with the picture's impressions of light and shade.

Art Nouveau and the Arts and Crafts movement inspired artists to link frames, either thematically or visually, to their painted image. For his Peacock

Room (Freer Gallery of Art, Washington DC), James Abbott McNeil Whistler designed an entire room as a 'frame' for his painting of *The White Girl,* 1862. Other artists sometimes emphatically extended the painted image: this is clearly demonstrated in the Symbolist works of Jan Toorop in the Kroller-Muller Museum, Otterlo. The sinuous, ribbon-like lines of the subjects continue directly onto the frames in etched grooves, echoing the engraving technique of early Renaissance engaged frames.

Another form of *trompe l'oeil* frame is seen in the Surrealist painting by Max Ernst entitled *Two children are threatened by a Nightingale,* 1924, (Museum of Modern Art, New York). Here, real wooden objects, a gate, house and knob are attached to the frame which now becomes a mechanical prop through which the characters threaten to emerge from their space into our own.

A great many twentieth-century works of art do not require isolating within a traditional form of border – indeed, they may not need a 'frame' at all. Numerous contemporary paintings are minimally, but entirely satisfactorily framed in thin strips of aluminium or wood, or sandwiched between glaze and backboard with clips, or hung in a simple perspex box (see plate 9).

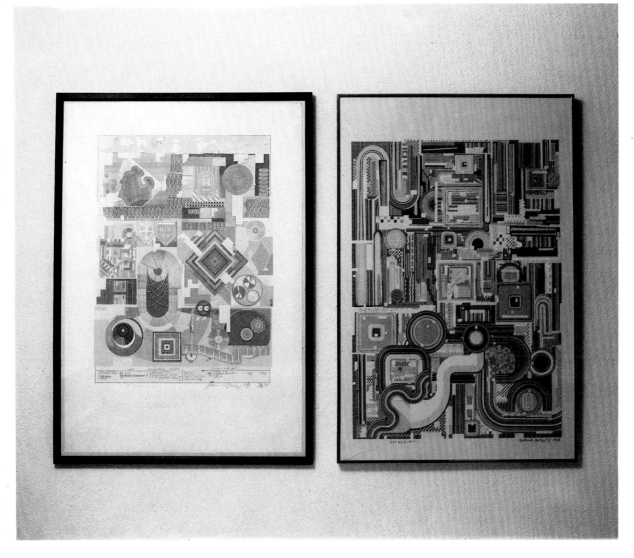

Plate 9 Eduardo Paolozzi (left) *Calcium Night Light: The Children's Hour* 1974–5, 105.4 × 76.2 cm (41½ × 30 in) and (right) *Untitled* 1974, 104 × 70 cm (41 × 27½ in), Private Collection

In the presentation of prints, particularly since the eighteenth century, the frame itself is usually very narrow and often has no decoration. Its purpose is to delineate the boundary of the real frame which is the wide margin of unprinted paper. This border—its size and its colour—is determined by the artist and is therefore totally integral to the picture. This fact is reinforced by the appearance of the border colour in the unprinted areas of the composition. Only when a print is removed from the folio to be displayed on the wall does the need arise for an external frame — to provide support for glazing and hanging. For these Paolozzi prints, the frames (one aluminium and the other ebony) are reduced to lines crisply demarking their space on the wall.

In the experimental art of this century, whether Cubist, Abstract or Conceptual, the frame seems to have two options: either to be fully integrated into the work of art itself or to disappear, being superfluous or irrelevant. Total integration occurs when the frame is treated as one of the elements that make up the work; in Pablo Picasso's *Nature morte à la chaise canée* (formerly in the artist's collection), the oval rope acts both as a link with the chair and as a descriptive border. Complete exclusion of any recognizable frame came with the departure from traditional rectangular, circular or oval shapes into the irregular profiles of works by artists such as Frank Stella and Richard Smith. It follows from the breakdown of the frontiers between painting and sculpture — with three-dimensional objects on the walls and flat objects on the floor (such as Carl André's *Bricks,* 1966, in London's Tate Gallery) — that it is obviously as impossible (and as contradictory) to put frames around such twentieth-century object-paintings as it is to put them around sculpture. These works do not require a frame either physically — to present and protect them — or philosophically, since they do not operate on the level of 'The work of art is an illusion. . .' We may conclude that our original idealist concept that picture and frame should be aesthetically inseparable has been fulfilled during the last century more than at any other time.

23

The Framer's Workshop

Although a workshop or spare room is ideal for framing pictures, a minimum of space will serve the purpose provided that it is well organized. Make sure that the workroom has adequate ventilation, especially if you are using strong-smelling or toxic substances such as stains and varnishes.

A bench or table with a flat surface and firmly-planted legs is essential. It should be positioned to receive either good natural light or well-directed light. An adjustable lamp clamped to the table edge is very convenient as it can be moved according to the job in progress. If the table- or bench-top is uneven, a sheet of thick chipboard of roughly the same size can be put on top to provide the necessary solid, flat surface, and the rough edges covered by binding them with adhesive tape.

Tools and equipment should be easily accessible but not cluttering the working surface, as the maximum of free space is needed in which to manipulate the picture, and stray implements can cause unforeseen damage. An arrangement of shelves with labelled boxes or drawers is useful for keeping tools and smaller items such as nails, screws, picture hooks and tape; a small second-hand bookcase could be adapted easily for this purpose. Essential sundries, often needed in a hurry, should also be kept close by. These include cotton rags, cotton wool (cotton), steel (wire) wool, a selection of brushes, screw-top jars for mixing paint or stain, spare knife blades, sandpaper of various weights, and jars of water and pure turpentine or white spirit (turpentine substitute). Small tubes or jars of wood filler, either plain or coloured, are needed for filling nail holes or missing sections of mouldings.

Extra shelving space should be set aside to keep mounts (mats), frames and pictures safe while you are getting on with other jobs. There is nothing so frustrating as finding spots of paint or wood stain on a mount which was left carelessly to one side on the bench while the frame was being coloured. To prevent such accidents, use large spare pieces of cardboard on the working surface and interchange them according to the job in hand. One card can always be used for, say, colouring and staining frames, to be replaced by a clean piece when dealing with a mount or picture, especially if the work has to be laid face down for measuring.

Many basic household tools are suitable for picture framing but some special tools are also necessary. These vary enormously in type and price. The professional framer's equipment is very expensive and not necessary for the amateur who only wishes to frame a limited number of pictures. Cheap tools, however, are generally unsatisfactory, as they deteriorate quickly and do not give a consistently good finish. As with most crafts, you should be prepared to spend money on quality materials if you want to get the best results.

Left: At the work bench. Jonathan Savill of The Rowley Gallery, London, sanding the corner of a frame. The working space is conveniently arranged with a shelving system to hold the smaller items such as nails, brushes and tools. Brackets projecting from the wall are ideal for hanging half-finished frames to keep them out of the way while work is in progress.

Below: The various tools used to make picture frames: a steel ruler b set square c electric drill d contour gauge e tenon saw f tack hammer g adjustable ruling pen h trimming knife with replaceable blades i screwdriver j bradawl k glass cutter l and m painting/palette knives n pliers o metal mitre box p mount (mat) cutter q scissors r lining fitch brush s flat bristle brush.

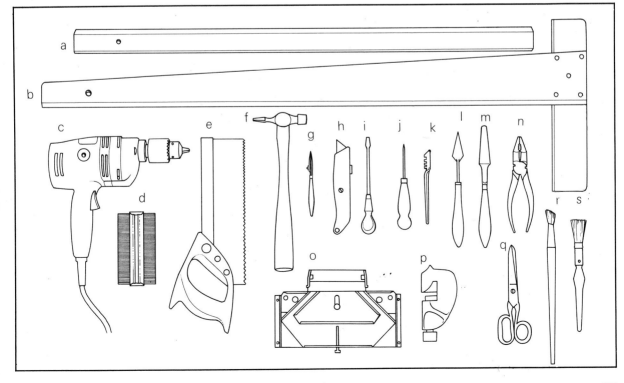

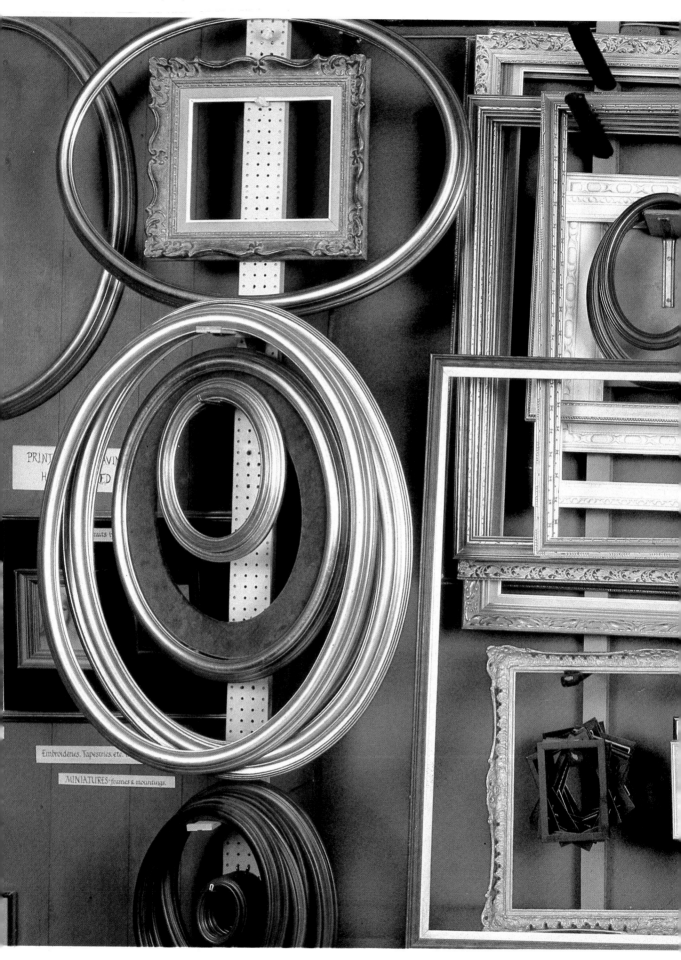

Perhaps the most essential tool for picture framing is the mitre box in which the moulding pieces can be clamped and cut at a 45° angle. Of the various types available, the most common and least expensive is the wooden box. Unfortunately, in time these frequently become damaged as the action of the saw causes the grooves to work larger, so that the necessary 45° angle-cut will no longer be·perfect and the corners will not fit exactly. Some of these boxes are, however, fitted with stay-pieces on top to prevent the saw from slipping. I personally prefer a slightly more expensive all-metal mitre box with two clamps which is more stable and thus ensures greater accuracy. The mitre machine used by professional framers is an expensive piece of equipment and takes up a fair amount of space, but it could be a good investment if you intend to do a lot of framing. The strong metal blades form an inverted V-shape set at a 45° angle, and the cutting action is controlled by a foot pedal, thereby obviating the use of a saw. Look around local shops to compare the different kinds of mitre box and ask the salesman's advice. You will find various tools advertised in art or craft magazines, with sources of supply.

When using the conventional mitre box, a tenon saw with small, fine teeth is required to achieve a fine edge on the angle-cut of the moulding. The saw should be deep enough to penetrate the wider or deeper mouldings, and outspan the depth of the mitre box. A panel saw should be used for cutting board where greater freedom is needed.

Use a good large, solid vice with a wide, deep clamp when joining the parts of frames. The ideal kind can be screwed onto the bench-top. Its gripping part should be lined with fabric or card to prevent the metal from marking the wood of the frame.

The ideal hammer for picture framing is one with a small flat head. This is most useful when putting backs on pictures as it does not slip about when the backing nails are hammered in horizontally. For heavier hammering or pulling out old nails, use a clawed hammer.

A steel ruler is essential for measuring and cutting mounts and glass. The best type has one straight edge to a depth of 6 mm ($\frac{1}{4}$ in), and the other side is lightly bevelled. It is infinitely preferable to the thin, flat kind when cutting mounts and, although quite expensive, will last a lifetime. Because of its weight, it is easy to hold firmly in place with one hand while cutting the mount with the other. The end of the rule which has a hole can be fastened to a sheet of thick chipboard, 13–20 mm ($\frac{1}{2}$–$\frac{3}{4}$ in) with a butterfly (wing) nut and bolt device, so that it can swing backwards and forwards while the other end is gripped during use.

With a little practice, glass cutting need not hold any terrors. Keep the cutter, either diamond or ordinary type, well oiled when in use. The wheel, which must be keen and sharp, will not become blunt until it has been used a great deal, after which

Left: A selection of made-up wooden and gilt frames in oval and oblong shapes and various sizes.

it should be replaced. Some glass cutters contain as many as six sections of wheel which can be used in rotation.

A light electric drill is ideal for joining the corners of frames as it allows one hand to hold the two corners of the moulding together. Make sure that the drill bit is the right size for the nails being used. Similarly, ensure that the size of the nail punch, used with a hammer to embed the nail below the surface of the frame, fits the size of the nails being used. The hole is then stopped and touched up to give a clean finish to the corner.

The best knife for picture framing is one with changeable blades. Of the different types, the most useful are: the knife with single, double-ended steel blades, with a handle that unscrews so that the blades can be turned round or replaced; and the knife with a long, sectional blade which is indented at 6 mm ($\frac{1}{4}$ in) intervals so that each section can be pressed off and a fresh section moved up to take its place. The latter is preferable for changing blades quickly when cutting a quantity of mounts, but some brands have blades which are rather thin and too flexible for work demanding greater pressure. Blades used for trimming and general framing jobs must not be re-used for cutting mounts where a razor sharpness is necessary to achieve a keen bevelled edge.

Most people will already have many of the other necessary tools and materials. Pincers and pliers are used for several tasks such as extracting stubborn, frequently bent and rusty nails from the backs of old pictures. Screwdrivers of various sizes are obviously indispensable for many jobs. A spatula and a palette knife make life easier when mixing paint, glue or other substances. Wood-worker's gouges, available in different shapes, are used for carving patterns if one is repairing an old frame. A small, strong bradawl with a sharp point is necessary when punching holes for nails or screws on the backs of pictures. Wire cutters are useful, though not essential as old but sharp scissors or secateurs will do just as well.

A plane would be very useful for smoothing down flat moulding lengths or removing an unwanted ridge from the moulding. Similarly, a medium rasp will smooth messy edges of wood or hardboard (masonite) when sandpaper is not strong enough. Clamps hold two surfaces together safely and firmly while they are being glued. A print maker's roller is particularly successful for flattening paper to a glued surface, and a painter's household sponge roller for laying glue on a large surface. A set square comes in handy for testing the right angles of a canvas on a stretcher, pictures, frames and mounts. Similarly a protractor is alway useful for measuring circles of a round mount, and a compass to check a correct angle degree.

A selection of brushes, all sizes and shapes, is essential for the numerous jobs in framing. At least one of these should be a large, say 5 cm (2 in), flat bristle, suitable for gluing or pasting. A lining fitch brush made of semi-soft bristle, with its flat, half-V shape, pointed at the end, is ideal for painting the recessed lines or profiles on frames. All brushes should, of course, be cleaned immediately after use to keep them in good condition. Almost equally useful are a number of different coloured fibre pens, and a lining pen and pencils for various tasks, such as marking measurements or drawing lines on mounts.

A strong adhesive, like polyvinyl acetate (PVA) commonly sold as wood-worker's glue, will serve many purposes, including joining the corners of frames, laying prints onto board and sticking down some fabrics. A simple starch (wheat flour and water) paste is suitable for laying down buckled paper-based work onto card or repairing tears in damaged paper (see Project 5). There are many adhesive tapes for different tasks: brown paper with gummed side (in widths from 2.5–7.5 cm or 1–3 in) for sealing the backs of pictures; masking tape (not the transparent type, as it exudes rubber solution which stains paper and cannot be removed) for attaching paper to mounts; double-sided tape for many tasks such as 'tip-mounting'. Stamp hinges are preferable for anything delicate or of great value where a minimum adhesion is required.

Different types of glass are essential picture framing equipment. Picture glass, known as 18 oz, is about 5 mm ($\frac{3}{16}$ in) thick. It is lighter and thinner than window glass which is normally 24 oz. Glass merchants (glaziers) will readily cut it to any size which is useful if you need only one piece, but it is better to learn how to cut glass yourself (see Project 2) if you intend to frame many pictures.

Non-reflective (or non-glare) glass is an expensive alternative, costing roughly three times as much as plain glass. It has a stippled or textured surface which diffuses the light in different directions, giving a dull finish instead of a shiny, flat one. Such a surface is especially effective for pictures hanging on walls that receive much reflected light. Non-reflective glass is quite acceptable on broad, boldly-coloured work set directly beneath the glass where the slightly blurred effect caused by the glass does not disguise any detail, but not for intricate work such as thin line drawings, etchings, pastels or anything with subtle variations of texture or colour. Also, any picture with a mount will not be directly against the glass but set slightly away from it, and fine details will be lost because of the distortion caused by the opaque quality of non-reflective glass, especially when the picture is observed from a side angle rather than straight ahead. Many people are unaware of this and may be disappointed by such a result.

Perspex (plexiglass) is another expensive alternative. It is lighter than glass, however, and flexible and unbreakable, which makes it useful for large-scale work such as screens. Disadvantages are that it marks and scratches fairly easily which, in time, reduces its clarity.

Pictures behind glass need a flat, firm backing as protection, to prevent dust and moisture from seeping in, and to keep them flat up against the glass so that the picture and mount do not warp. The backing, usually of hardboard, is nailed in horizontally as described in Project 2. Small head-less brads are normally used for this job.

Many different types of clips and screws are used for attaching pictures to frames. Diamond-shaped glazier's staples are quick and easy to insert with a glazier's staple-gun, but are only suitable for smaller pictures. Swing clips (turn buttons) are used when a removable back is needed, such as on a photograph frame where the small metal clip is screwed into the back so that it can swivel round. Spring clips are also used to enable a picture to be removed more easily as in Project 1. Flat glass plates are best for old or delicate stretched canvases when the canvas and frame-back is the same level (see Project 10).

The choice of hanging fixtures depends on the size and weight of the picture. Screw eyes, with or without a second ring, are the most commonly used hangers. Back hangers are attached to the backing board rather than the frame, the pins being inserted through the holes, then bent under as described in Project 5. This is an ideal solution when a heavier picture has a frame too thin to take a screw eye without danger of the wood splitting.

Back hooks are excellent for large frames holding very heavy pictures or mirrors. Otherwise, glass plates can be used to attach these straight to the wall, in which case you may need to drill the wall-holes and use long nails with rawlplugs (screw anchors) for safer and firmer gripping, especially if the wall is a plaster surface on hard cement or brick backing.

It is most important to use a good quality stranded picture wire of the right thickness for the weight of the picture. Brass chain can be used for hanging very large pictures or mirrors. Such chain can form part of the overall decorative effect in older houses where there are picture rails. Otherwise, a satisfactory wall hook is the type combining a hook with a sharp nail inserted through it, made in three sizes, the largest being double with two nails which is strong enough to carry heavier frames.

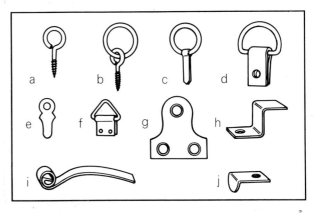

Above: A selection of hanging fixtures: a *screw eye* b *screw eye and ring* c *back hanger* d *D ring* e *swing clip* f *back hanger* g *glass plate* h *and* i *steel clips* j *spring clip.*

Below: An 'exploded' drawing of a frame

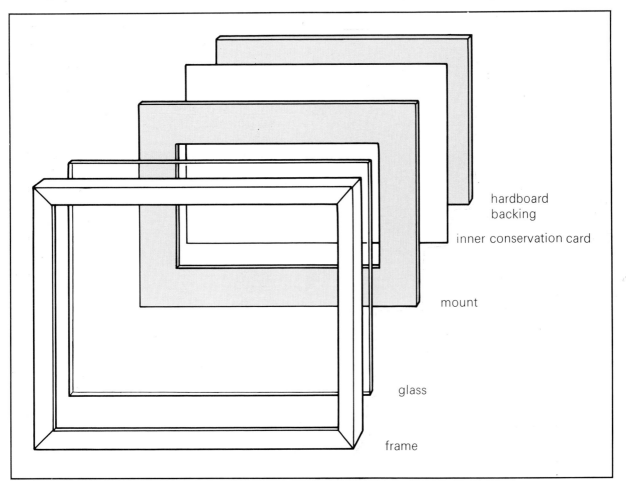

hardboard backing

inner conservation card

mount

glass

frame

Mouldings
and Finishes

Wooden mouldings with a cut-out or rebated (rab-beted) edge are available in a variety of shapes from wood merchants, hardware, do-it-yourself and craft stores and some retail picture frame suppliers. They can be bought by the length which varies between 2–4 m (6–15 ft). Hardwoods such as oak, ramin or jelutong, and softwoods like pine, are most commonly used for mouldings, although elm, mahogany, ebony and others are equally successful if a little more difficult to obtain. Ramin is a pale wood with little grain apparent, oak has a streaky grain, and pine a pronounced grain with knotting patterns.

As well as basic wooden mouldings, some hardware merchants also carry a range of ready-finished mouldings. These vary from the simple, smooth, black-lacquered type in flat or rounded shape of 1–2.5 cm ($\frac{3}{8}$–1 in) wide, which are popular for certificates or photographs, to plain white and colours sometimes relieved by a tiny gilt edge. They also include wider, more ornate shapes with plaster or plastic base, either painted or with a gilt finish, modern or 'antiqued', or mixtures of paint and lacquer. Some of these commercial mouldings can be quite satisfactory, depending on the object to be framed, but others tend to look rather cheap and 'mass-produced'. Whereas wholesale moulding is generally supplied only to professional framers in bulk (comprising several hundred metres in one order), some manufacturers do sell moulding direct to the public in lengths of about 4 m (12 ft).

Moulding shapes vary from the perfectly simple to more elaborate sections with a number of varying planes in the contour, as illustrated here. The most usual shapes are flat, round, spoon, box (sloping inwards), convex, concave, reverse, and any slight variations of these. They range in width from 1 or 1.3 cm ($\frac{3}{8}$ or $\frac{1}{2}$ in) to 7.5 cm (3 in) or more for either a plain contour or a more complicated one. Basic shapes can be added on top of each other or to more elaborate contours to achieve an interesting result known as a 'composite' frame.

As most raw wooden mouldings are mass-produced and the quality of the wood varies, moulding bought by the length frequently has not only a rough surface but even pieces missing. Try to avoid such damaged sections when cutting out the frame. Small imperfections should be rubbed lightly with medium weight sandpaper to remove the rough surface and the excess dust wiped off before a stain, paint or wax is applied. Knotting effects or distinct grain-lines can, however, enhance certain pictures, particularly paintings of the 'primitive' type where the crude style blends well with the rough wood to create a feeling of rustic simplicity.

The natural wooden look for frames has recently regained popularity and can be seen on a diverse range of subjects including old, coloured prints and the modern, highly-decorative indigenous Oriental paintings collected by travellers. Old, natural wood frames in simple flat or gently sloping shapes were originally used on etchings and engravings of country scenes, 'genre' or pictorial paintings from the Victorian era. The original frames, to be found occasionally at auctions or in second-hand shops, are highly prized, especially those made of unusual wood which is difficult to obtain today. Some of them will have been so stained and polished over the years that the original grain has become lost under accumulated layers of brown stain and polish. However, as described in Project 10, this can be carefully removed to reveal the distinct quality of the wood.

A detailed explanation of how to measure frames is given in Project 1. To estimate the amount of moulding needed for a frame you have to examine the piece you intend to buy and calculate roughly how many sides can be cut from one length of moulding, remembering to allow extra for the angle corners and also for any faults that appear in the wood. It may be more difficult to plan how much to buy for a bigger frame as not so many sides can be cut from each length. In this case you may have to buy an extra length for only one side, and so have a lot over. However, it can always be used up later for another frame or for experimenting with colouring and staining.

Many and varied are the ways of treating wooden mouldings – with stains, paints, gold or silver leaf, waxes or varnishes. An imaginative framer will be continually searching for new ideas and combinations of colours and materials.

Wood stains are oil, spirit or water based. The colours can be intermixed to form subtle variations or diluted with the appropriate thinner (turpentine, methylated spirits or water) if the tone is too strong. Hardware and paint shops have a great variety of colours ranging from pale oak or teak browns through to mahogany and black and including subtle shades towards green or grey. Colour charts, available in most stores, will help you choose the most fitting shade, but remember that the depth and tone depend very much on the type of wood to which the stain is applied. A hard, close-grained wood, for instance, has a slower rate of absorbency. Test the exact stain by dabbing it on the back of a piece of moulding rather than the front, to avoid wasting a section of the wood if the colour happens to be unsatisfactory.

Whereas transparent stain sinks into the wood and merely enhances the natural finish, opaque paint conceals the grain and texture of the wood unless it is diluted. Wood stains are often available only in a restricted range of earth tones, so there is

Left: Four Victorian pictures in period frames.
The Cornfield, *a coloured print by G. Baxter, in the traditionally popular gold mount and frame, has a black bevel on the mount to set it off. The other print,* The Rustic Bridge, *has a reproduction carved brown frame and silver slip with polish giving it a warmer tone. The thick black lacquered frame with tiny gilt inner edge around the sampler is typical of late nineteenth-century domestic framing. A more unusual frame is on the eighteenth-century sepia engraving* The Happy Mother *by Bartolozzi. Its gesso base has been stained and 'antiqued' to resemble tortoiseshell, and it has a fine gilt filigree edge.*

usually a greater choice of colour when using paint. The most suitable paint for colouring frames is acrylic which can be applied straight, or diluted with water so that the wood grain is still visible. This latter finish is suitable for soft water-colours where a mild and unobtrusive result is needed to reflect the painting. Applied in its ordinary consistency paint will cover the grain completely so that the moulding serves only as a base for the colour. In this case it may be necessary to give the frame more than one coat of paint to make sure that the wood is entirely covered. Such a flat paint finish is suitable for paintings, pastels or drawings with a lively and expressive character. Choose a colour already in the picture, not necessarily a dominant one, but one with enough representation in the picture to justify its being repeated in the frame.

One step further than a plain paint finish is a 'paint on paint' effect, created by adding a layer of contrasting coloured paint to the first colour after it has dried, then rubbing it back carefully with steel (wire) wool so that the under-colour partially shows through. The exact way of doing this is described in Project 5. Many combinations are possible: blue upon red will give a purple effect while retaining the original qualities of the colours; similarly, green upon red will yield a brownish effect overall, but in both cases the result is more interesting than a flat purple or brown.

An alternative to acrylic is lacquer paint, obtainable in small jars. This has a limited range of bright colours which can be intermixed and, because of its shiny appearance, there is no need for a wax or varnish finishing coat. It is sometimes used on a simple, rounded bead type of moulding for Chinese or Japanese prints. A variation is a gold base with the lacquer applied over it and then rubbed back, as for the 'paint on paint' finish, to reveal small streaks of the gold.

Another attractive finish, known as 'liming' (see Project 6) combines wood stain with paint. It is a stain base with an additional light, diluted coat of acrylic paint which is rubbed back to reveal the underlying stain, leaving a residue of the paint in the grain of the wood. This combination provides a subtle, more restrained finish than plain paint on paint. It is therefore suitable for work where the colours are soft and harmonious, so that a gentle blend of different shades are repeated in the frame from the painting. A relatively wide frame with several planes in its contour can successfully

A variety of frame corner samples. Far left (from left to right): dark brown stain; soft gilt with grey rub; close-grained linen slip; black Hogarth with gilt edges; silver leaf; flat veneer with polish finish. Left (from left to right): plain pine with wax finish; polished maple with gilt slip; wood with 'bamboo' treatment and silk-covered centre; plain gilt; stained wood with stained burr-elm veneer centre and gilt-rubbed edges; gilt with broken leaf finish. Above (from left to right): gilt with dark green painted centre; gilt with red rub; plain silver leaf; stained brown; lacquered black; silver leaf with stained polish; dual-grey paint rub with gilt ridge.

Mouldings and Finishes

Right: A successful combination of modern pictures—prints and drawings—in unpretentious surrounds and older oil paintings in ornate gilt frames provides a harmonious setting for the antique furniture and ornaments in this comfortable room.

combine a limed finish with additions such as a plain colour on the inner edge, or a vivid line added to an upper ridge to give definition to an otherwise muted overall effect.

There is a great difference of quality and texture between the gold or silver leaf and the gold or silver paint used on frames. The leaf is composed of very thin sheets of metal several centimetres square and is generally applied to a smooth gesso or plaster base with a special glue size, although it is sometimes applied to wood which has been well sanded and sealed. The leaf is patted carefully into place and allowed to dry (see Project 9). It can then be 'antiqued', if necessary, and finally sealed with varnish. This gold/silver leaf has a distinct shiny finish.

The gold/silver paint is composed of a fine powder which is mixed with lacquer and thinners and applied in liquid form. It has a granular quality which disperses light in different directions so that the surface is duller than and lacks the intense sheen of the leaf gold. This gilt liquid mixture is easy to use as it is painted on and dries quickly. It is also available in small jars as a paste, known as gilt wax. A special varnish for use on top of either the paint or the wax can be applied as a sealer-coat and protective finish. Older frames with pieces missing or the gilt rubbed off can be touched up with either golf leaf or paint, whichever is the most appropriate.

A more unusual finish than paints or stains is a veneer. This is a sheet of thin bark which is cut into strips, dampened and when soft and pliable, glued onto a section of the moulding. The whole frame and veneer section can be left plain or stained, then waxed and polished. The burr-elm bark has a particularly interesting, knotted surface and, when stained lightly with a wood grain surface such as pine, the result is very pleasant. The word 'veneer' may suggest a machine-made appearance, mirror-smooth and heavily polished, but the bark itself, if treated carefully and applied by hand, will have a soft, natural finish quite unlike the laminated surface of some modern furniture.

Whatever the types of finish chosen, subtle variations can be achieved by mixing two or more paints or stains together. If a stain shade is too intense use an appropriate thinner to dilute it. Some colours, such as black and mahogany, are much stronger than others and caution should be used when mixing them with weaker stains. Paints also mix well, although it is more difficult to judge the exact shade which will result as the paint tends to dry to a different tone from that in its liquid form, and will darken after the application of wax or varnish. It is wise to test the paint on a piece of spare wood before committing a whole frame to an 'unknown' shade.

Above: Samples of stains, straight and mixed, applied to light oak moulding. Left column: natural wood; teak; red mahogany; walnut. Centre column: golden oak; light oak; medium oak; black oak. Right column: diluted black oak; black oak and rosewood; medium oak and rosewood; black oak and green.

Right: Cross sections of basic moulding shapes showing the simple rounded 'hockey', flat, concave and box types of varying width and depth, and the more elaborate contours which combine small ridges or beading with the general curves.

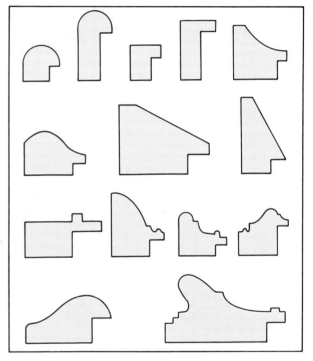

Make a rough estimate of the quantity of any colour combination needed for a particular job and mix enough of it to complete the frame, as it is almost impossible to match the exact shade again. It is a good idea to keep a record of the proportions of each colour as you add them together, especially if you have discovered a combination which you might like to use again, or need to repeat the same finish on a series of similar pictures but may not be framing them all at the one time. Store the mixture in an airtight screw-top jar with the recipe of the proportions attached to the front of it. Provided the jar is firmly sealed the colour will keep for some time.

Before beginning work on a complete frame you may first wish to test the innumerable ways of treating wooden moulding, with paint, wood stain, gold, silver, wax or varnish. Buy several lengths of moulding of different shapes and widths and experiment on small off-cuts of, say 15–30 cm (6–12 in) long, to get an idea of the various possibilities of colouring, staining and waxing. When you have experimented in this way and become familiar with the materials, you will be ready to consider the colouring and width of frame in relation to a particular picture. This is not as easy as it may at first appear.

Placing a painting on a support such as an easel or on the floor against the wall and fitting coloured moulding samples onto it will enable you to decide on the most suitable frame. By moving backwards and forwards from the painting you will gain a sense of the proportion for size and a sense of perspective for space. It may also help if you place other unframed pictures of varying sizes side by side and observe the different results when moving the samples from one to another. You will thus recognize the sympathetic or discordant elements. Certain colours and tones may need to be lightened, darkened or intensified according to the individual picture, and only a slight change may be needed to bring frame and picture together.

Right: Modern reproductions of older styles of frames. A selection of round and oval shapes in gilt and stained wood, a hand-carved and gilded Chippendale, two Hogarth frames — brown and black with gilt edges, and maple with gilt slip.

When a frame has several different planes within its contour, it may look rather flat and insipid in one overall colour; whereas adding variety can bring it to life. A successful combination of colours is created when the tones range from the lighter on the inner or rebated edge to the darker on the outer edge; the small lip of the rebated edge can be quite strongly contrasted to the other more softly graded tones of the rest of the frame. Whether the frame is a simple section or a more elaborate one, it can be enlivened by imaginative finishing touches. Add a contrasting colour to the inner edge, or paint a thin line of colour along a channel or recession in the contour or on the prominent ridges to accentuate them. An overall spatter or spotting effect, or a slight 'antiquing' will reduce a bold colour to suit an older or more traditional type of painting.

A softly painted inner edge on a frame combined with a limed centre and a top ridge rubbed with gilt wax makes a suitable frame for many oil paintings or

Below: A softly-contoured stained wooden frame with a light polish provides an ideal surround for this old woven picture of a sailing ship in muted colours. Samples of the type of wool used for the weaving are shown in the foreground.

water-colours. An otherwise plain, stained frame can be given an original look by extending a painted line from the inner edge to the first ridge, but the colour should be considered carefully as this is the part of the frame which divides it from the picture so the colours should be compatible. Gilt or silver wax can be rubbed onto the inner ridge, applied lightly so that the base colour shows through to avoid a heavy or sharply defined edge. If a more distinct edge is needed, gold or silver leaf can be applied. Felt tip (fibre) pens are an easily available alternative, are simple to use and come in a variety of strong colours. Additional colours such as these should be added with caution. It is easy to be over-enthusiastic and an excess of finishing touches can make the frame look precious and over-worked. Such a result will inevitably distract attention from the object to its surround, thus destroying the unity of the frame and the picture.

Below: These two fine etchings by Christopher Penny would look elegant in any setting. The clean lines of the aluminium frames against the neutral colour of the wall sympathize with the simple contour of the bookcase whose white colour repeats the paper surrounding the prints.

Mounts

A mount (mat) provides a pleasant, restful area of space between a piece of art and its surround which prevents the picture from looking squeezed into the frame. It also encourages the eye to travel inwards across the mount to focus on the object. Glass placed directly over such defects as wrinkles and creases always tends to magnify them but stretching or 'straining' paper into a mount helps to keep the picture taut and flat.

Mounts are particularly effective with watercolours, drawings, pastels, prints and any works with a paper base, especially those not glued onto a support. Less valuable pictures or prints can be glued onto cardboard satisfactorily, but many old prints, water-colours or modern lithographs should not be glued down or trimmed because they immediately lose their value. (Also, at some future time, a picture may need to be cleaned or restored which will be made doubly difficult if the picture is glued firmly onto a support).

Pastels should never be fitted straight into a frame as particles of the pastel, although treated with fixative, may stick to the glass. Over a period of time such action can be exacerbated by humidity in the atmosphere. I have seen an old pastel removed from its frame leaving at least 75 per cent of the picture on the glass. Even a thin mount will provide just enough space to prevent the pastel from coming into contact with the glass.

Mounts can be made from a variety of materials which suit different types of pictures, but card is the most popular and easily obtainable. Mount card is made in varying thicknesses; the one used for most mounting purposes is of 8 sheet, approximately 3 mm ($\frac{1}{8}$ in) thick. Sometimes a thicker card is required to give a feeling of greater depth, and if one of sufficient bulk is not available, two pieces of card can be glued together then cut in the normal way.

As it is not always possible to find the exact colour of card needed, an alternative is to buy a piece of paper of the correct shade and glue it onto cardboard. Art shops sell a large variety of papers, such as hand-made, or rice-papers, and marbled patterns, with many subtle colours and textures which complement different kinds of pictures. A slightly grained texture combined with a soft, mottled tone, for instance, can greatly enhance water-colours, drawings and coloured etchings. The paper can be glued onto card quickly and easily by using a spray-pack adhesive and a print-maker's roller, an ordinary rolling-pin or just a large wad of cotton. Spray the adhesive evenly on both surfaces, then carefully lay the paper onto the card and smooth out by hand, working from the middle to remove any air bubbles. Continue to flatten the paper with a roller or cotton wad, being careful to distribute the glue evenly, not forcing it all outwards.

Valuable pieces of art should be mounted only with conservation board, also known as 'museum board'. The use of this card is recommended by all reputable conservators, museums and galleries. It is made entirely of rag which is acid-free, whereas the ordinary types of card are made from wood pulp which can, in time, encourage stains or marks to appear on the picture. Museum board is available in specialist art-paper stores. It is, however, obtainable in only a limited colour range, usually white, ivory or pale grey, but it is possible to buy good paper also made from rag and glue it onto the board. In this case, a pure wheat flour paste (see page 89) should be used instead of the spray-pack adhesive.

Fabric mounts can supply an unlimited range of colours, richness and individual textures which card lacks. Chinese or Japanese woodcut prints and Indian or Persian miniature paintings, for instance, are enhanced by silk mounts whose refinement and subtlety of texture complements the subject matter. In the same way, the richness of velvet can greatly benefit photographs or miniature paintings with a ceramic or ivory base. A large range of linen fabrics is available, from fine-grained cotton to coarse hessian (burlap) and wallpaper-like textures which can be used to great effect on broad water-colour landscapes, portraits or modern prints. Unusual mounts made from leather or suede – either real or simulated, provided it is of reasonable quality – add lustre to portraits or old master reproductions.

To choose the right colour, tone and width of mount is not always easy and, obviously, much depends on personal taste. Sometimes a mount which we imagine to be suitable looks wrong when actually fitted to the picture and framed. This is because it is hard to visualize the finished effect, especially for beginners who are not aware of the many variations of mounts and framing.

The right colour is very important. Dark mounts tend to send the eye inwards towards the picture more than lighter ones, especially when the picture is lighter in tone, but too great a contrast between picture and mount should be avoided, except when a deliberately dramatic effect is wanted. Many people think of mounts in limited terms of white or cream, grey, sepia or black. Perhaps they are either unaware of the range of possibilities or afraid to use other tones or colours for fear of making a wrong choice. In fact, there is a lot to be said for 'playing safe' because a particular effect can soon become tiresome, especially if the framing tends to absorb more attention than the picture, and it is easier to live with something neutral and unprovocative.

Some useful colours for mono- or hand-coloured etchings with brown or green tones such as hunting or country scenes, old buildings and churches are: various olive greens, bottle green, shades of brown from tan and mushroom to sepia and chocolate, and shades of green-grey. Water-colour landscapes and seascapes with predominant blue or green tones may need softer and paler shades: off-white and cream through to warm beige, pale grey and blue shades, pale green to grey-green shades.

In all cases, the spirit of the picture itself should first be considered – whether it is bold in colour or design, extremely delicate in colour or linework, or

Left: A range of mount corner samples in a variety of colours and materials, including plain and textured card, fabric and several with line and wash treatment.

somewhere between the two. A modern abstract with vibrant shades may benefit by having a strongly coloured mount of a contrasting colour to create a dynamic, vivid effect. A less striking picture is often much harder to mount satisfactorily; on a medium-toned picture a mount of a similar tone can look dull and flat, whereas one of stronger tone can be too dominant. There are various subtle ways to relieve this monotony by using coloured lines, line and wash treatment, a small fillet or 'under' mount to make a double mount, and coloured or gilt bevels.

To help in selecting the most suitable shade of mount, make a rough template of two or more corner pieces of card in several tones, dark, medium and light, which can be fitted against the picture. Place the object on a table and hold the corner pieces so that it is 'framed' or surrounded on two or more sides by card to give you an idea of the finished effect. If the subject of the picture is 'floating' in its own surrounding space, say a print of a bird, animal or flower on a white paper background, hold the corner pieces together in a position halfway between your eyes and the picture. This will help you decide on the inner size of the mount, that is the amount of space to be left around the actual picture. Move your template backwards and forwards in this way until the most satisfactory proportion is found.

Choosing the appropriate width of mount is not so difficult, as it is simply a matter of holding the mount card against the picture and then putting various moulding samples along its edge. Proportion is obviously the major consideration here, as it is a pity to cramp a picture with a mount which is too small. Generally, a picture of about 50 x 40 cm (20 x 16 in) can take a 6.5–7.5 cm (2½–3 in) mount. Smaller items such as photographs may need no more than a width of 3.8–5 cm (1½–2 in), depending on their size. This is, of course, just a guide, and various individual paintings or drawings will demand more unusual proportions. Some modern lithographs, for example, need spacious mounts, even though the print itself may be comparatively small, and these are often set in quite a narrow frame which provides a contrast. The mount and frame should be different widths, because a frame as wide as the mount will look heavy, especially if it is darker than the mount. Also, if mount and frame are the same width, the repetition of lines can be irritating by drawing attention away from the picture.

Most mounts are the same width and depth on all four sides but in some cases, such as traditional oriental paintings or scrolls, the borders are wider at the top and bottom than at the sides. Some pictures benefit by having a larger border at the bottom only. This should be barely noticeable, no more than 6–15 mm ($\frac{1}{4}$–$\frac{5}{8}$ in) more than the other three sides. It does, however, provide the picture with a visually solid base which is not apparent until it is actually hanging on the wall to be observed from a distance.

Pictures on interesting paper with hand-hewn edges or old manuscripts with uneven or torn edges which should not be covered, should be 'tip-mounted' onto a backing of card, rather than having a cut-out mount. This means simply attaching the

Above: This red mount with two different sized 'window openings' provides a dramatic colour contrast to the simple black script on white of this calligraphy by William Blake. However, the strong effect is modified by the plain gilt frame.

Right: A group of coloured etchings with six different mount types; they include fabric mounts and mounts with fillets as well as line and wash.

object to the card with stamp hinges or tiny pieces of double-sided tape (see Project 5), leaving the appropriate width of mount around the picture on all sides. Stamp hinges are advisable if the picture is valuable, as they can be removed easily and without harm. The glass enclosing it on the front and a firm backing will keep the picture flat.

For a picture where both sides are interesting enough to be visible, such as a double-sided manuscript or water-colour from a sketch-book, it is possible to construct a double-sided mount and enclose it within two frames with double glass, back to back (see Project 7). This type of frame is known as a glass trap.

Once the choice of colour, shade and size of mount has been made, it is time to consider other ideas to help improve the relationship between mount and picture. We have previously touched upon the possibilities which could brighten an otherwise uninteresting mount, especially if the picture is rather dull in tone and needs to be given a 'lift'. A single coloured line added to the mount on the inner edge, only a few millimetres from the bevelled edge, can do a lot to overcome the abrupt change between mount and picture. Use a shade

which is repeated in the image itself. A black, gold or coloured ink can be perfectly acceptable, but pencils or sharpened conté crayon are equally effective. A conté line would, for instance, be appropriate to a conté drawing of the same colour.

Some pictures may need more than one line, perhaps only two, one slightly thicker than the other.Many variations are possible, using different colours, but it is advisable not to overdo it. Bear in mind that the lines should not be too heavy or noticeable but blend with mount and picture. Experiment by inserting lines onto template corner samples and holding them against the picture.

One step further than individual or even double lines is to make an arrangement of several lines with a band of soft water-colour added, which provides an extremely attractive 'bridge' for some water-colours. This combination, described in greater detail in Project 2, needs a mount of at least 7.5 cm (3 in) wide, or else the whole effect will look pinched. It is mainly suitable for larger paintings, although some very small pictures look pleasant with a wider mount finished in this way. If it is a small picture, the width of wash and number of lines should be kept to a minimum, as it is easy to 'crowd' a small painting. Keep the colours subdued to avoid drawing attention away from the picture.

Another effective addition to a mount is a band made of self-adhesive golf tape. This can be either plain or 'antiqued' with a light stippling of wood stain applied with a brush and allowed to dry before putting it on the mount, positioned near the inner edge in the same way as a line or wash channel. A different finish is achieved by applying the tape to the bevelled edge. Painted bevels can look striking in either white, black or in a contrasting colour.

Mount cutting is described in detail in Project 2. Use a knife that has strong changeable steel blades which will not bend under pressure. Although the mount can be cut with the knife held straight, a 'bevelled' or inward-sloping edge gives a certain finesse. Thicker card will obviously yield a more pronounced bevel than a thinner type. The knife is held flush against the edge of a steel ruler placed on the drawn lines on the reverse of the card. It is then pressed in so that it penetrates through the card and drawn down the length of the line while the other hand holds the ruler firmly in position.

A fillet or double mount is made by cutting an inner mount to fit under the main mount so that only a small part of it is showing. This combination gives a definite lift to an otherwise monotonous appearance. Because of the narrow width of the inner mount – ideally it should be between 2–10 mm ($\frac{1}{8}$–$\frac{3}{8}$ in) – a brighter colour is acceptable and, as usual, a most effective combination is achieved by choosing a colour that is repeated throughout the picture.

It is possible to take this idea further and have a 'triple' mount. Make sure that the chosen colours complement one another and the picture, and also manage to avoid the confusion which could be caused by a multitude of lines. This latter problem can be overcome by cutting one or other of the mounts with a 'reverse' bevel. The mount is cut in the same way as described in Project 2 but with the card face up rather than cutting from the back, so that the bevelled edge slopes inwards and under – in other words, the bevel is hidden. Thus, two mount colours are side by side without the interference of a white stripe between them.

Alternative Frames

The large range of alternative framing methods now available has made it easy to select a cheap and appropriate means of displaying pictures without going to the trouble and expense of making or buying conventional frames. To frame inexpensive prints and souvenirs, the majority of commercial framing packs are far better than using drawing pins, adhesive tape or plastic putty as a temporary measure, because paper work hung up in this way deteriorates quickly. Regular visits to do-it-yourself or art stores, picture framers and junk shops can produce stimulating results for the non-purist in the search for both 'non-framing' methods and the numerous ready-made frames.

The conventional four-sided frame with mitred

corners can be replaced for certain types of pictures by hanging fixtures comprising individual components which are fitted together. They are available in kit form with instructions for assembly which are easy to follow. These simpler types of display are suitable for such items as decorative reproduction prints, and where a minimum of fuss is appropriate. As less expensive prints are not intended to have as long a life as more valuable ones, the beauty of these self-assembly frames is that they can be taken apart easily and the picture replaced by another.

One particularly effective and inexpensive way of displaying less valuable pictures is the glass, back and clips method. This consists of a 15 mm ($\frac{5}{8}$ in) of chipboard and a sheet of glass cut the same size. The picture is sandwiched between the glass and the board, then held in place by clips made of either metal or strong, clear plastic, one side screwed into the board, the other edge overlapping the glass at the front. One or two clips per side are used, depending on the size of the picture. The screw-holes should be placed so that the component pieces are held together as a firm, tight section, but remember that the clips will take only a certain thickness of glass combined with paper, so a mount (mat) may prove too thick to be included. If intending to use thicker components, be sure to buy thicker chipboard — 20 mm ($\frac{3}{4}$ in), but it does weigh a lot more and should be hung with care.

Another useful, decorative way of enclosing a fairly small picture or photograph between glass and backing, is simply to use *passe-partout* tape to bind the edges. Very popular a few years ago, *passe-partout* has gone out of fashion since the introduction of new types of tape. Available in many colours its main advantage is a tough, hard-wearing finish. However, other types of tape can be substituted, and many of these are prettily patterned. The *passe-partout* method is unsuitable for larger or heavier pictures, because the tape may not hold the weight of the glass.

A double-sided picture such as sheet music, a cover from an old magazine or a piece of decorative script, can be put in a 'glass trap' between two pieces of glass for display. This type of hanging is described in Project 7. A free-standing glass trap with a slit wooden base for the object is equally attractive for treasured cards or photographs with messages on the back. Three-dimensional articles such as fans, creative collages or embroideries, look most effective in a 'shadow box' setting, the glass raised away from the item by fillets or an inner frame, as in Project 8. Posters and reproduction prints can be simply glued onto chipboard or hardboard

Left: Glass and clip framing fixtures and several ready-cut mounts. The corner-brace system with string attached for hanging is seen from the reverse, next to a small picture assembled in glass and clips with a board backing. Separate components of glass, board and clips are shown before assembly. The three mounts are from a large range in various colours, with oval or rectangular centres, single or with fillets.

(masonite) as in Project 3, using the same principle as the 'block-mounting' done professionally where the paper is glued and sealed in one operation by machine, the protective sealer coating the surface.

Metal (aluminium or brass) frame kits are popular for lithographs and modern prints. Artists especially find them convenient for temporary use in exhibitions as the work can be easily removed and replaced. Metal frames are useful for larger pictures because they are very strong, and their simple, clean lines make them suitable for modern works.

For lighter work, with or without glass, hanging brace fixtures are most suitable. Consisting usually of four corner braces with string joining them together across the back of the picture, these simple devices are effective for hanging pictures on board, paintings on canvas or small mirrors. The string is pulled up tightly into a central ring which also serves as a hanger and the object is thus held secure.

Even simpler are the pieces of thick bent-over plastic strips, available in pairs of various sizes from most shops selling reproduction prints. The top of the picture is held neatly and firmly in one strip and the bottom in the other. String is inserted on the inside of the top strip along its length for hanging. As these plastic strips do not carry weight heavier than

a thick paper print and certainly not glass, this is usually a temporary form of display, frequently used for hanging calendars, rubbings or posters. If the print has been rolled up for some time and/or is slightly buckled, it will not hang flat against the wall and should be first flattened using a cool iron or placed between boards for some time with a weight on top.

Wooden rollers, for hanging scrolls or embroideries perform a similar function. The 'picture' is attached to the rods at top and bottom with staples or nails, and simple or decorative wooden or metal knobs are fixed to the ends of the rollers to give a finished effect. As wood is heavier than plastic, the object will lie flat against the wall. Take care in aligning the picture correctly when fixing it to the roller, otherwise it will hang crooked. If you do not want to nail the piece of material to the rollers, secure it by loops of matching fabric, sewn over the rollers to the back of the hanging. Fold a paper-work scroll over the rollers in the same way, but secure it by using strips of matching paper and a suitable paste or adhesive.

Another simple surround used mainly for oil paintings on stretched canvas is known as a 'baguette'. This is not strictly a frame but four flat,

found in all department stores, some stationers and branches of large chain stores. Being mass-produced they are cheap but not very imaginative and are best for framing photographs and cards. They come in stock sizes and serve a useful purpose as they are fitted with glass, swing-clips (turn buttons), strut backs (easel backs) and hangers. However, the range of colours is very limited, mainly black, white or gold, and the available shapes are generally only square or rectangular.

Second, and more interesting, are ready-made frames in various shapes and sizes from picture framers. Those in raw wood can be coloured or stained for perhaps a small oil- or water-colour where one or several shades in the picture can be repeated on the frame. Many framers sell odd frames originally ordered by their customers then later cancelled or simply not collected, but do not be so thrilled by your 'bargain' that you purchase a frame which is the wrong size for your picture.

The third section covers the vast range of reproduction frames which vary in richness of quality, design, size and shape. The growing popularity of smaller, more intricately detailed paintings and miniature portraits is catered for by numerous miniature frames made of metal, brass, stained or

Left: A selection of aluminium kits comprising the various components, and pictures in ready-assembled frames. The etching Mont St Michel *by Barry Owen Jones has a wide cream mount with a narrow aluminium frame. A brown acrylic kit frame is seen from the reverse to show the corner joining system and the hanging fixtures.*

Above: Two glass traps containing butterflies. The plain box frames are covered in decorative adhesive paper, and are suspended from above on invisible nylon thread so that they can be viewed from either side.

Right: An old shadow box containing a collage of carefully blended grasses, ferns and seaweed. The heavy wooden frame has obviously been stripped of paint or layers of stain and varnish to reveal the interesting wood grain, and lightly polished.

wooden sections without rebates (rabbets) or mitred corners. These are nailed along the four sides of the stretcher with each end overlapping the following side for a neat effect. The nails are driven slightly below the surface of the wood, filled and then retouched as described in Project 1. This is a cheap and satisfactory way of concealing rough sides of canvas nailed on a stretcher and supplying a neat, unified appearance for a picture which has enough impact of its own and does not need a more elaborate frame.

If, for some reason, you are unable to make many frames yourself, do not be afraid to use and adapt some of the ready-made frames of different types, sizes and prices which are available from various sources. These can be divided roughly into four sections. First, there are lots of 'instant' frames to be

gilded wood, in round, oval or rectangular shapes, plain or elaborate, modern or antique. Examples are the Italian Florentine designs, gilt on red base with engraved line-work and foliate corners, and the Victorian miniatures with wreath and ribbon patterns. All these little frames are usually supplied with flat or convex glass. If the size of the frame does not fit the picture, a larger one can be chosen and a card or fabric mount inserted, which can sometimes make a definite improvement.

Reproduction frames are not confined to the

smaller sizes, and indeed may range up to 70 cm (28 in) or more. Such large-size ovals are useful for full-scale portraits, drawings or paintings. To make these frames more individual you can add 'profile' lines to tie in with the colouring of the picture (see Project 7), or lightly 'antique' an over-bright gilt by dulling the sheen as described in Project 6. Such frames make excellent surrounds for mirrors and some are sold as such.

Genuine antique frames are, of course, less easy to find and can be very expensive. To the untrained eye there is little difference between the real hand-carved and gilded wooden frame and plaster moulded on wooden base with a gilt finish. By scraping a small area with a sharp blade in an unobtrusive part of the frame, you can soon find out what it is made of. Solid old wooden frames have a pleasant, warm feeling of seasoned timber very different from the modern unseasoned greenish wood. These are worth cleaning up and preserving as described in the next chapter.

Below: The largest of this group of small frames and miniatures is no more than 18 mm (7 in) across. Different materials incorporated in these frames include metal, gold leaf, black lacquer, burr-elm veneer and velvet.

You may think it worthwhile to cut down an unusual old frame to fit a smaller picture, but this is best avoided if possible. If the painting is proportionally smaller than the frame on each side, why not make a slip or liner to fit between frame and picture instead of making the frame smaller? Such an addition sometimes sets off both the picture and the frame. The slip or flat section could be wood, gilt or linen. It must be an exact fit to bridge the gap between picture and frame. Inserting a slip is certainly preferable to cutting down in the case of an ornate or swept frame because of the risk of the wood splitting or the plaster breaking away. If you must cut such a frame, hold the sections nearest to the corner while sawing in order to help prevent splitting. Otherwise, fabric can be bound tightly around the section and taped together; adhesive tape should not be used directly on the frame to bind it as the surface finish may be lifted away when the tape is removed, especially if the frame is gold leaf.

Care and Restoration

All paintings, drawings and prints need as much regular care and attention as other room furnishings. Many pictures of value or otherwise suffer through unintentional neglect, perhaps left in the same position on a wall for some time and consequently taken for granted, or stored in a spare room unnoticed. Pictures which have been hanging for a long time accumulate dust and dirt, the frames become brittle with age, the fixtures may rust and the cord or wire deteriorate. Check the fittings occasionally to make sure that they are firm and strong. It is also wise to check a picture which you have bought ready-framed if you intend to hang it without alteration, especially if the framing is old.

Pictures in store, whether framed or not, can suffer from various hazards such as dampness, often combined with warmth, conditions which encourage mould and paper buckle. Paper-based work is also vulnerable to insect attack, especially as some types of glue used in the past for mounting pictures are a great attraction to moths and silverfish. Art on paper without a frame should be stored on a flat, dry surface with intervening sheets of tissue-paper, preferably in a strong cardboard folder.

Oil paintings, whether canvas- or board-based, can develop blistering, flaking or mould caused by the same type of atmospheric conditions; the paint film lifts away from the base and the surface of the paint shows a faint 'bloom' or misty patching. If storing a large number of paintings on canvas, do prevent them from knocking together. When many pictures are stacked together it is worthwhile to place sheets of stiff card or board between each one.

A light dent in canvas can usually be removed by gently moistening the area on the back with cotton wool dipped in water. As the canvas dries it will contract and flatten out. Dents left for a long time, however, may not flatten out easily. Old paintings on brittle canvas are hard to flatten, and damping the canvas back may cause damage to the sized base or the paint structure as the water seeps through to the front of the canvas. Instructions for repairing a hole or tear are given in Project 10.

Any picture or frame being moved from one place to another should be regarded as fragile, even though it may not be noticeably so. A charcoal or pastel with a loose-textured surface, a flaking or blistered painting or an old ornate frame, may all suffer a sudden knock or bump which can dislodge particles or pieces. Packing pictures for long-distance travel obviously necessitates expert advice from a reputable specialist in picture removal, but normal day-to-day removals need only a few precautions. Most professionals store and transport their frames with wads of corrugated card pinned or taped to each corner. These protect the corners,

Left: This well-preserved gilt frame is a typical example of the elaborate framing popular in the Victorian era. The shell and scroll patterns harmonize with the elegant portrait and the finely painted details of the dress. The effect is enriched by having an oval rather than rectangular opening to the frame.

particularly if the frame is ornate, and act as a buffer for the rest of the picture if it comes up against other objects. If mailing prints or soft paper-work, carefully roll the paper and put it in a thick card cylinder with metal cap-ends.

There are many methods of maintenance and cleaning to combat the various perils which threaten different types of pictures. First of all it is important to carry out a general surface clean by dusting pictures and frames carefully, and cleaning the glass. You can then judge whether more extensive work is necessary, such as restoring paintings or prints, and repairing and retouching broken frames. Valuable pictures should be cleaned and restored only by an expert, but simple surface-cleaning and patching can be done by an amateur, provided that great care is taken.

Framed pictures should be removed from the wall before being dusted and cleaned. Harsh abrasive cleaners must not be used on frames as they are likely to damage the surface by removing the protective varnish or wax and possibly attacking delicate gilding underneath. A rag dampened with water to which a few drops of household detergent have been added will remove surface dirt from frames, but there is danger of water seeping under the glass and onto the mount (mat) or picture. Use a commercial window cleaner or methylated spirits for the glass on framed pictures, as such liquids evaporate quickly with no danger of seepage, whereas water tends to leave smear marks on the surface.

For more extensive cleaning, it is necessary to take the picture and frame apart. You can then examine the components and decide which needs to be replaced. Amazing results can be achieved by simply taking an old water-colour, etching or print out of its frame, perhaps giving it a new mount, dusting and cleaning up the separate pieces and refitting them all.

It is not worth the trouble to refit pieces which are beyond cleaning or badly damaged. If the picture has obviously been framed a long time ago, all the components may be brittle so the job must be done carefully. Pull out rusty old backing-nails slowly so that they do not split the wood. Unless the backing-board is still in good condition, solid and unwarped, it should be discarded and replaced. Years ago, there was a tendency to use pieces of rough wood to back pictures, sometimes two or three separate pieces for one backing, and the gaps between each piece allowed dust and moisture to enter. If there was no intervening card the resin from the wood often stained the paper in streaks. Such stains are not easy to remove.

Lift out the old picture and examine it carefully. An old, discoloured mount will need replacing, although I have known individual cases where the mount was considered valuable enough to be cleaned because it bore the artist's own writing. Apart from such incidences, it is not worth trying to clean an old mount which may not respond well to the usual bleaching treatment. It is quicker and easier to cut a new one. Also, the fragile thin paper layer on old card may lift if subjected to moisture.

Removing an old mount from a paper-based object can be difficult and should be done with great care. Both the card and the paper may be brittle and the paper, especially, could tear. If the picture is joined to the mount with brown tape, it is simple to cut lightly around the edges of the picture with a sharp blade where it joins the mount (the slight ridge will be visible through the paper), and separate them. Removing the half-side of tape attached to the picture will need particular care, especially if the paper is thin.

Transparent adhesive tape (such as sellotape or scotch tape) should never be used for attaching pictures to mounts as it has unfortunate results such as staining and wrinkling which are often hard to remove. Old stains caused in this way may be covered up unless the inner or bevelled edge of the mount is barely covering the edge of the picture.

Another problem occurs when mount and picture are glued together. Flour paste used to be applied to a mount at a distance of 6–13 mm ($\frac{1}{4}$–$\frac{1}{2}$ in) from the inner edge. Such paste (described in Project 5) may become brittle with age, drying out in a crusty layer. This makes for easier removal, as sliding the fingers inwards between the mount edge and the picture will part them. Otherwise, a blunt spatula or palette knife can be inserted.

If a new mount is to be cut (see Project 2), the measurements of the old one can be used as a guide. These measurements should be checked first for accuracy, as the plate-marks on an etching may have been covered up, or the proportion of the mount may be wrong. However, re-mounting an old picture may prove awkward as you will be used to seeing it in a certain surround. Whether suitable or not, the old mount is familiar and it may be hard to decide on a new one. There may be a brown stain around the picture where the original bevelled edge fitted over the image, and cleaning will either remove this entirely or at least make it less noticeable.

After the picture and mount are removed, look at the glass in the frame. Glass on an old picture gathers dirt inside as well as out. Although it can be cleaned, you may be disappointed to find, after much scrubbing of odd marks, that there are some defects such as scratches, pitting or spots which are irremovable. Unfortunately, these will show up even more clearly after the rest of the surface is cleaned, especially if the picture has a fresh, clean mount. Old glass was the 'rolled' type often with ripples and distortions as we can see in window glass of that time, and these effects will also be more pronounced when the glass is cleaned.

Now to the frame itself: dust which collects around the inner, rebate (rabbet) edges if the backing is loose should be removed with a stiff brush. After refitting the picture to its frame, it is most annoying to find specks of dust between glass and mount. To avoid such 'foreign bodies' dust all the component pieces before fitting them together.

Before the framing is completed, check the four corners. The nails may be loose and need tightening, the corners may have split and, if the frame is thin, it will not be worth repairing. There should be more than one nail to join each corner, even on a thin frame. I have seen frames that had obviously been joined by gluing only and without nails, so that when the glue dried out over a period of time and lost its adhesion, the frame collapsed. This is more likely to happen if the picture is heavy and/or contains glass. Corner nails need a solid surface to grip effectively, and a dilapidated corner will not be strong enough, even if cracks are strengthened with wood filler.

Old, warped frames or stretchers can be braced so that they will hang flat against the wall by nailing a flat, solid piece of wood to the back of the frame. Ideally, this batten should form a cross, one piece slotted into the other, the four outer points being screwed firmly into the frame.

More time can be wasted on repairing than on making a new frame. The thinner rebate edges of small frames are prone to splitting, and these are often not worth mending if there are pieces missing. However, it is worthwhile repairing stronger or larger frames by mending splits, reinforcing corners or rejoining corners and using new nails.

Cleaning and restoring an old frame (described fully in Project 10) can be interesting and satisfying, but may take some time. After the initial cleaning, any sections missing from ornate moulding have to be carved to the right shape and retouched. If the damage is extensive, with a crumbling plaster base, cracks and missing pieces, the frame will continue to deteriorate as it is being handled. If you ask a professional to refurbish old frames which are in very bad condition, do not be surprised when the estimate for such work seems unusually high: the framer can foresee the amount of time and concentration needed and, in professional terms, both are expensive.

Retouching damaged frames can be very much a matter of improvisation and feeling for the texture as well as the colour. Whether the original frame is gold paint or leaf, wood stain or paint, with or without a varnish, a spattered or 'antique' finish, you may need to experiment, depending on the surface. Large areas on a frame which is obviously gilded with metal leaf should be retouched with patches of gold leaf not paint, otherwise the repair will be conspicuous because of the difference in the patina.

Old frames with a thin, veneered surface such as maple, in simple flat or slightly rounded shapes were popularly used for hand-coloured country scenes during the last century. These frames are very different from the modern reproductions which have a smooth laminated surface. Very often the pattern of the grain is hidden by layer upon layer of brown stain and varnish as the frames have been polished and repolished. It is not difficult to remove the accumulated layers by rubbing the frame with a rag soaked in methylated spirits, replacing the rag as it picks up the sticky varnish. If the varnish is obstinate, a light abrasive action with fine steel (wire) wool will help. Previous repairs may appear as the surface is removed. Cracks and holes in the veneer can be covered with a special wood filler as des-

Above: A coloured print by G. Baxter. Foxing is evident on the picture, particularly in the sky area and around the inner edge of the old mount. The old gilt frame has been knocked and parts of the corner pieces have broken away, as is clearly seen in the detail on the left. But the discoloration can be treated and the moulding restored.

cribed in Project 10, after dabbing some PVA adhesive into the recesses. Stick back any pieces of the veneer which fall off in the same way. Once the frame is cleaned, dried and patched, you may want to change the colour or darken it with a wood stain. As wood stain is transparent, the pattern of the grain will still show through it. After this has dried, a varnish can be applied for a shiny finish or beeswax for a lighter, softer sheen.

The original 'Hogarth' frames (see page 37), which became popular in the eighteenth century as surrounds for fine black and white engravings, are often worth repairing as they have a solid appearance which the mass-produced copies lack. The dull gold filigree edges (sometimes with a hand-carved base) bordering both edges of a rich, dark centre, can be restored quite easily. Missing pieces of the gold edges can be replaced with barbola paste and retouched with gilt wax. The grimy central black area can be darkened with black wood stain and repolished as necessary. These frames have probably softened in colour with age, so the retouching should also be soft and subtle.

Old oil paintings on canvas stretchers should be taken down from the wall and examined from time to time. To brush away accumulated dust on the back of the stretcher, the canvas may have to be removed from the stretcher as described in Project 10. If there is any sign of wood-worm holes, blight (fungus) or wood shavings, treat the stretcher with a suitable insecticide in the same way as when treating frames. However, if the stretcher is a rough one and in otherwise poor condition, it may be best to renew it completely.

Holes made by wood-boring insects are unsightly and may cause the eventual disintegration of the frame. A frame with evident holes may have been treated in the past with insecticide, but if the attack is recent, the holes will look fresh and exude fine dust. The damage caused by wood-worm spreads rapidly below the surface as a series of small tunnels running this way and that, not visible on the surface except as tiny round holes, and by the time these have multiplied enough to be conspicuous the damage below the surface is extensive. More importantly, untreated wood-worm in one frame will soon spread to your furniture and, over the years, to the very fabric of a house with wooden floorboards and roof timbers.

As soon as a few holes are visible the picture should be removed and the frame treated with a special wood-worm insecticide. The wood should be thoroughly and generously doused with the liquid, using a full brush. Use out of doors if possible, but if indoors there must be plenty of ventilation. Covering the whole frame is important, even the areas with no evidence of holes. The liquid will soak into the wood gradually, but a second application may be necessary. Allow the wood to dry out thoroughly before any other repairs or refitting of the picture takes place.

I once dealt with an oil painting on a wooden panel which had several recent wood-worm holes. In this case, a syringe was used to inject the solution into each hole separately, to avoid possible damage to the painting. The holes were afterwards filled with a mixture of insecticide powder added to beeswax, and later retouched.

Old pictures, whatever their medium or support, will suffer the ravages of time. Pictures which were once subjected to the fumes and smoke of open fires using coal now have to contend with the dry atmosphere of central heating, a modern hazard which sucks moisture from the air and can cause oil paintings to blister and buckle, lifting the paint layers away from the base support. Most oil paintings have a light, transparent film of varnish for protection. Certain types of natural resin varnish such as mastic or copal tend to become brittle, to change colour and darken with age, hiding subtle details under layers of varnish and dirt. Sometimes varnish has been added layer upon layer with the mistaken idea of brightening the picture up, but

actually having the opposite effect.

It is a general practice to remove such varnish and replace it every twenty-five years or so without disturbing the underlying paint. This operation should be done *only* by those with experience and knowledge of varnish-removing solvents and their diluents. The quicker-acting solvents, especially, can penetrate through the varnish and remove the paint, unless the action is arrested by the counter-action of the diluent. Delicate nuances of colour formed by an over-glaze technique (soft, transparent washes of colour pigment mixed with varnish) or scumbling technique (a slightly more opaque layer of colour pigment) can easily be removed at the same time as the varnish if they are not recognized as being glazes. However, it is possible to remove surface dirt from an oil painting without removing the varnish itself (see Project 10).

A reliable and popular picture varnish is made from dammar resin, a natural, soft resin which is very durable and less likely to darken with age than the resins mentioned above. It should be applied in a warm, dry atmosphere as any dampness in the air is likely to encourage 'blooming' – moisture trapped in the varnish, causing opaque, frosty patches to appear later. Dammar crystals can be bought from artists' suppliers and mixed with equal parts of pure (distilled) turpentine. Place the crystals in a bag of muslin or other porous cloth and suspend it in a glass jar with the turpentine, then cover with a tightly fitted lid. Leave for several days until the crystals have melted, stirring occasionally.

Apply the varnish to the painting in a draught-free atmosphere so that dust will not settle, as particles and bits of fluff will be very noticeable in a shiny, clear varnish after it has dried. The mixture should be spread on thinly with a soft bristle brush, using criss-cross strokes. Brushing out the varnish with a backwards and forwards motion in this way will render the surface less shiny.

A combination of this varnish with beeswax will give a softer finish. It is made by mixing four parts of the dammar varnish (made as above) with two parts beeswax and one part pure turpentine. These are heated together in a double saucepan (the lower one containing hot water, so that the mixture is not over direct heat) until the wax is dissolved. When cooled slightly, the mixture can be stored in a jar. It is applied with a lint-free cloth, allowed to dry and then polished.

Unvarnished paintings suffer from attack by air pollution, general dirt and fly-spotting, all of which can cause changes of colour to the paint through chemical reactions, and these pictures are much harder to clean. Paper-work can be particularly fragile and subject to deterioration. A water-colour may fade and the paper may turn brown, if placed in direct sunlight. Different types of paper suffer in varying degrees from humidity, dampness and insect attack. Hand-made paper is more durable and less likely to change colour than machine-made paper which often has a high acidic content likely to cause it to turn brown (sometimes in a very short time), and it will also become brittle to the touch.

The brown spots known as 'foxing' or greyish mould blotches which appear in paper can be cleaned and sterilized with a solution of bleach, as described in Project 6. However, the nature of the art-work must first be taken into account, and the exact method of cleaning determined according to the type of work. For instance, water-colours, ink, charcoal or pastel drawings and others where the colour or surface texture is endangered by immersion in water, should be treated with great caution.

If the wood of the frame is soft and, perhaps through having the screws put back in the same hole over the years, the wood is split, the screw will work loose and must be replaced. Always make new holes when fitting fresh hangers.

The nails on which the pictures hang should be put in at an angle, especially to take the weight of heavier pictures, and also so that there is less likelihood of the picture wire slipping off the nail. The type of nail with hook attachment is ideal as the nail is designed to be driven into the wall at the right angle.

Below: The old maple frames do not overpower the delicate lines of these four coloured prints of fishes, and the gilt slips provide light relief.

Project 1
Basic Frame for a Painting on Canvas or Board

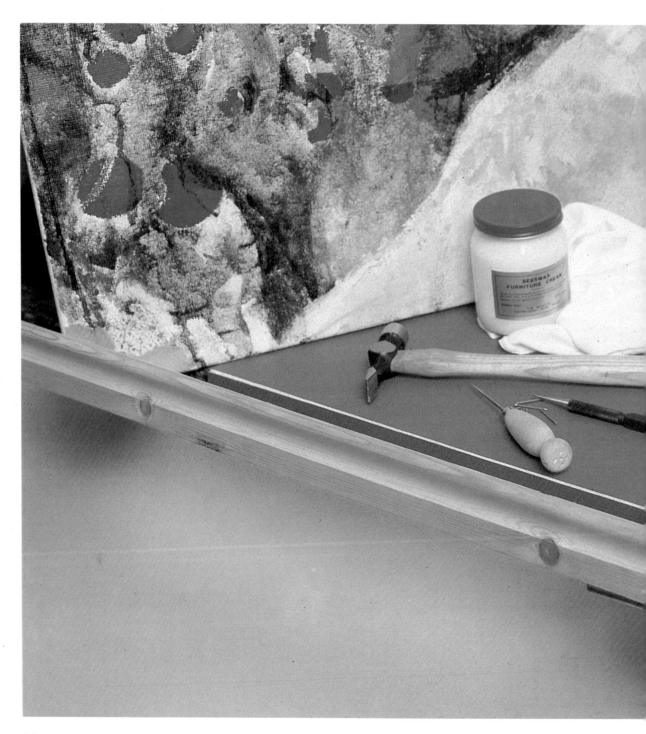

Every amateur painter or student has an oil or acrylic on canvas or board which needs some kind of surround to provide a neat finish and also a support for the hanging fixtures. The simplest type of frame is often quite adequate for such a painting, and its construction provides the opportunity to learn the principles of framing.

Always try to select and create a frame that suits the painting in size, shape and colour. Some paintings, whether large or small, need little more than a plain, narrow frame whereas others will benefit from a more elaborate display. Surprisingly, perhaps, a wide moulding may look very effective on a small picture where a narrow one would be insignificant. An older painting, or one with richer or darker colours will be able to take a more ornate frame, perhaps with gilt or silver undertones and an antiqued finish. Modern abstracts will look better with shape, size and colour kept to a minimum.

The majority of paintings falling mid-way between modern and older styles are fairly broadly painted and often vivid. They may be impressionist landscapes, flower paintings or still-lifes. The most suitable frame for these may be one which combines different colours with several planes, depending on the complexity of the design and colour in the picture. Paintings which have soft or subtle shades may take either a frame of strong contrast or one that echoes the colours of the picture and acts as an extension of the painting itself. For instance, a bowl of multi-coloured roses may have a reddish tint occurring throughout the composition which could be repeated as a soft line on the frame. Similarly, a bright seascape with dappled colouring may provide a thread of blue or green for use on the frame.

The large acrylic on canvas to be framed here is a semi-abstract, the subject matter including flowers against a background of hills and sky. As the composition is brightly coloured and decorative, the most suitable frame would be one that does not detract from the painting. A 5 cm (2 in) wide moulding in soft pine with a pronounced grain and knotting at intervals was chosen, as its simple lines and country character were in keeping with the spirit of the painting without being too strong for it. The shape is a spoon moulding incorporating a rounded upper edge curving down and inwards to a small bead and fillet on the inner edge.

In this case, it was decided to leave the natural colour of the wood for the frame, as the light, warm buff tone complements the various colours in the picture. An alternative would have been to choose a wood stain from the range of earth colours, although any of the browns would be too strong as there is very little definite brown in the painting, whereas there are gold tones which blend well with natural wood. The shape of this moulding would lend itself well to a combination of colouring: for example, the addition of a different shade to the middle curved space, a line of colour on the bead ridge, or a contrast colour on the inner fillet edge. In this case, however, the one overall shade does not detract from the rather colourful image.

Although left plain, the pine will need the protection and nourishment of a varnish or wax. All types of wood, whether hard or soft, should be preserved in this way. If the painting has a matt or softly-waxed surface, a waxed frame will provide a similar surface to blend both picture and frame together. Typical examples would be an impressionistic type of unvarnished oil painted broadly and simply onto a canvas with a coarse weave, or a 'primitive' or child's painting in similar style, where a matt frame often relates more easily to the picture

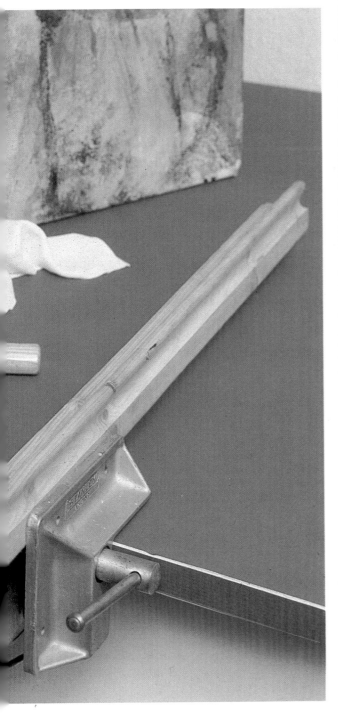

Left: Two moulding lengths of the pine frame gripped in the vice after being nailed together, with various tools and part of the acrylic on canvas in the background.

Step 1

Place the canvas on a flat surface and measure it from edge to edge, allowing for any protuberances such as tacks on the sides or linen folded at the corners. Measure each side in at least two places to ensure accuracy in case the canvas is not exactly square. Add at least an extra 2 mm (1/16 in) but not more than 13 mm (1/2 in), depending on the size of the rebate, to each measurement to ease fitting the canvas into the finished frame.

Step 2

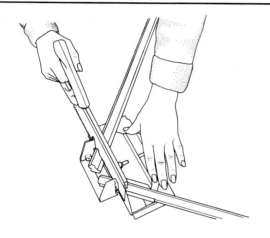

Mark the measurements exactly onto the length of the moulding and clamp it firmly into the mitre box with the pencilled marks lined up on the angle-cut. Some mitre-cutters, like the one shown here, cut two pieces of opposite angles simultaneously. The moulding must be positioned firmly and straight, otherwise the corners will not cut at a perfect 45° angle. Saw through the two pieces, and repeat for the other corners.

Step 3

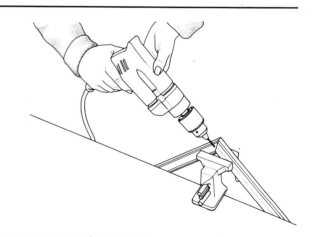

Fit two pieces of moulding together in the vice so that they are gripped tightly and the corners meet exactly. Drill holes – at least two, or three if the moulding is wide – through the corner of the first section and well into the second, but avoid boring the holes too close to any edge, especially the rebated edge.

Step 4

With the nails hammered in and the frame now joined, grip one corner of the frame in the vice. Support the other part of the frame if necessary. Hold a nail punch on the nail-head and tap it with a hammer to sink the nail not more than 3 mm (1/8 in) below the surface, but enough to hide the head so that the hole can be filled.

than a hard shiny one. A light wax is also the most suitable finish for the frame illustrated here.

After selecting the type of moulding, you will have to estimate the amount or number of lengths you need to buy. Moulding comes in various lengths: some are as short as 1.5 m (5 ft) while others are as long as 3.7 m (12 ft). Measure the painting (Step 1), then calculate the measurements of the four sides of the frame, adding enough to each side to cover the angle-cuts, and a little more for wastage at either end of the moulding. You will obviously have no difficulty cutting a very small frame from one length of moulding, whereas a large picture may be harder to calculate. In any case, it is wise to buy more than you need.

The picture here is 116 cm (46 in) by 86 cm (34 in), and each moulding piece is about 3m (10 ft). It is therefore possible to cut two of the long sides from one length, and the two shorter sides from another length leaving some over which could be used for colouring experiments or making a small frame. If the moulding length had been shorter, say 2.5 m (8 ft), it would have been necessary to cut one long and one short side from each length of moulding.

Another way to measure a picture (apart from the rebate (rabbet) or edge to edge method shown in Step 1) is known as taking 'sight' measurement. This is not the overall size of the picture, but represents the visible area of the picture after it is framed. This measurement is normally used where a specific area of the painting needs to be shown, for example, when there is a signature very close to the edge of the picture which might otherwise be covered by the rebate of the frame. Another instance is when a stretched painting has rough edges, perhaps with missing paint-work, which are better covered. For the sight measurement, the inner point can be marked on the moulding and the 45° angle line extension marked out from it.

Many painted canvases on stretchers are not truly rectangular, especially if they have been badly stretched and 'keyed out' more at one corner than another because of the uneven tension in the material. Such paintings must be measured very carefully. If the picture is out of square more than 6 mm ($\frac{1}{4}$ in) on any side, there will be difficulty fitting it into a frame with a small rebate area. It is therefore wise to choose a frame with a rebate of, perhaps, 10 mm ($\frac{3}{8}$ in) or more, rather than one with a rebate width of 3–6 mm ($\frac{1}{8}-\frac{1}{4}$ in). A frame with a small rebated edge may not take a crooked stretcher which is out of square (on any one side) more than the rebate width.

Mark the measurements on the moulding pieces with a sharp pencil, so that the inner points, whether for sight or rebate sizes, can be extended to form the cutting lines for the mitred corners. Accuracy is essential, as even a fraction out will result in a non-rectangular frame because the mitred corners will not meet up in a perfect 45° angle.

The vice used for joining the frame must have broad grips and be firmly attached to the bench or table-top. Have the relevant joining tools to hand so that you will not be groping for them while in the middle of the job. A combination of glue and nails is necessary to provide a strong joint which will take the weight of the picture. Glue alone is not enough, even on a small painting, as over a period of time the glue may separate from the wood thereby losing its adhesion. The size of nails used is determined by the size of the moulding, but they should be headless so that they can be sunk below the surface of the wood easily. The nails must be long enough to penetrate right through one piece of moulding and half-way into the other at each corner. The number of nails for each corner depends on the thickness and width of the moulding: one or two will be adequate for a smaller moulding, but at least three, or even four, will be necessary for a larger one.

Position the nails in the thicker part of the wood. Take especial care in judging the right position when the moulding shape has a chunky portion which slopes away, as in some 'swept' types, so that the nail does not penetrate right through the thicker part and come out through the thinner part. Some concave shapes, such as reverse moulding (falling away and downwards from the inner edge) will need a nail inserted on the upper part, which will be visible from the front of the frame. Observing a cross-section of the moulding will help you to determine the exact position of the nails before drilling the holes.

If a light electric drill is used, it is possible to clamp the longer piece of moulding in the vice with the corner as close to the grips as possible, and drill the hole while holding the shorter piece in the other hand. The more usual household electric drill, however, requires both hands to steady it. In this case, or when using a mechanical drill, it is necessary to clamp both lengths of moulding in the vice, as demonstrated in Step 3.

First join the two opposite corners of the frame together, forming two L-shapes which can then be joined, rather than going around from one corner to the next. This will also ensure maximum strength in the frame because the nails on the adjacent corners will not be running in the same direction.

It is very disappointing to find that a mitred corner does not meet exactly after the nails are hammered home. Such unevenness can be avoided by holding the free piece of moulding slightly lower than the one in the vice while hammering in the nails.

Only a light smear of wood-worker's glue (PVA) is necessary on the inside of each corner before it is nailed. Any excess glue will be forced outwards by the pressure of the joint, and should be wiped away with a damp cloth, especially any on the upper part of the frame, before it dries. Because wood-worker's glue dries less quickly than some other adhesives, it is particularly useful for joining frames. If you intend to stain the frame, remember that the wood will not receive the stain if there is a hint of grease or a smear of glue. This will not be apparent until the stain is applied, when paler portions will be left at the corners. After nailing, the frame should be set aside until the glue is thoroughly dry to ensure maximum strength.

Once the nails have been sunk and the corners

Step 5

Sand the corners with the medium-weight sandpaper by drawing it carefully in one direction and towards the corner on each side, then softly up and down on the corner itself. This action will avoid catching up splinters. If slivers or chunks of wood do break away, the missing areas will have to be filled, sanded and then retouched.

Step 6

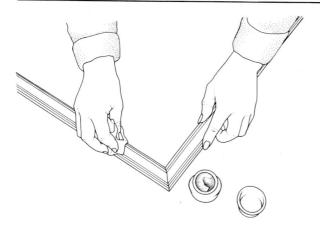

Sand the whole frame lightly to remove dust, dirty marks, spots of glue and excess wood filler at the corners. Apply beeswax fairly thinly but evenly with a piece of clean rag. If the wood is soft and porous, use a little more wax. When dry, the wax can be buffed up to a shine with a soft, dry cloth.

Step 7

Lay the frame face down on the table and slip the canvas into it. A canvas which is truly square should slip in easily with only a shred of space on each side. However, an unsquare canvas, such as the one shown, may leave uneven gaps on two sides. To prevent the stretcher from slipping about in the frame, cut small squares from a bottle-cork to the right width with a sharp knife. Insert them as padding where necessary between the canvas sides and the frame, against the rebate. A drop of glue on the cork will keep it in place.

Step 8

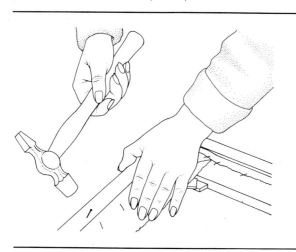

Hammer 3 cm (1¼ in) nails into the back of the frame, in this case two to each side and fairly close to the inner edge. One nail to each side would be adequate for a smaller picture. They should be sunk until you feel that they grip well into the wood. Lightly tap the nails over and inwards until the heads are touching the stretcher. The canvas will be kept in place, but it should be possible to remove it by twisting the nails around without taking them out.

sanded (Steps 4 and 5), look closely to see how much filling and retouching is necessary. The nail-holes should be stopped and any missing sections built up with wood filler which can be touched up after it has dried. Rub a small piece of the filler between two fingers to form a tiny roll, quickly fit it into the hole and wipe away the excess. This method prevents a messy or lumpy finish and lessens the amount of retouching. A little filler should be rubbed over the extreme edges of the corners to neaten them and prevent a ragged finish.

Methods of retouching vary according to the finish, the idea being to match the colour of the filled areas as nearly as possible to that of the frame. This is where a store of small jars containing mixed paints and stains comes in handy. Natural, plain stain or gilt frames, where you can dab on the liquid straight from the container, will obviously be easier to match than others. In some cases you may have to employ a dual effect, as with an antiqued gold where it will be necessary to paint the gold liquid or wax on first before stippling over it with a wood stain.

The difference between the colour of the filler and the wood on the pine frame was only slightly noticeable, so that it needed just a tiny amount of light oak diluted with thinners and dabbed on carefully to avoid spilling onto surrounding areas. As this was a fairly large and unwieldy frame, various marks and smudges had appeared during the making-up which had to be removed by a thorough sanding before applying the wax (Step 6).

Clear, colourless beeswax which is compatible with all types of wood was used here. It is made by mixing the wax lumps with turpentine, in the proportion of one part beeswax to three parts turpentine. This mixture is heated in a double saucepan (not over direct heat) until the wax melts, then allowed to cool. It will form a soft paste, which can be stored in a jar. The wax is applied sparingly with a lint-free cloth, allowed to dry and then polished. If you cannot obtain beeswax, there are various colourless commercial waxes available which can be used as alternatives. Wax is soft, remember, and may not withstand being handled, so that frames finished in this way are easily damaged if knocked.

An alternative to wax is a coat of clear lacquer which will give a really tough finish to protect the frame, but even a slightly tinted lacquer will alter the colour of the wood to a darker or more golden shade (as in the case of a liquid french polish). If you are at all unsure of the result, test the lacquer on a small off-cut of the same wood before applying it to the frame. The very shiny lacquer polish finish may be too bright, but it can be brought back to a softer matt by waxing over the polish once it is thoroughly dry. Remember, however, that you cannot apply a lacquer or spirit polish over wax.

Before fitting the canvas into the frame, clear the work surface and put a clean piece of card or material on top to prevent damage to the frame when it is laid face down. When easing the stretcher into the frame, check carefully to ensure that there are no gaps between the edge of the picture and the frame. Any such gaps will be at once evident if you stand looking straight down onto the canvas from above. Pieces of cork (as used in Step 7) can be cut to the exact width of a small gap when the stretcher fits more crookedly at one end of a particular side than at the other. However, if the gap extends a long way, an alternative is to insert slim fillets of card, a good solution for a picture which has a signature so close to the edge that it would otherwise be obscured by the rebate. It is important with a large frame (such as the one shown here) not to force the padding material into place, especially towards the middle of the length, as the long sides may bend under pressure, resulting in the edge of the stretcher not being concealed by the frame. This may not be noticeable until the picture is hanging up and the wall behind is visible through the thin crack.

There are various ways of attaching a stretched painting to its frame. Although it is common practice to drive nails through both stretcher and side of canvas into the frame at an angle, the nails are often so sunk into the soft wood of the stretcher as to make them very difficult to remove later. Not only is there danger of tearing the canvas when the nails are removed, but the nails have often rusted with age. Here, the nails are driven into the frame, not the stretcher (Step 8).

Spring clips are ideal for securing a painting on either canvas or hardboard (masonite) when the level of the back of the picture is below that of the frame back. These clips are screwed into the back of the frame, one or two to each side, and the 'spring' part curves inwards and down to rest against the back of the stretcher or hardboard to hold it in place. The picture can then be removed easily by swinging the clips up and around.

When the reverse occurs and the back of the canvas projects a little beyond the back of the frame, there is another type of clip which also screws into the frame: this has an angled metal leg to fit over the back of the stretcher and hold it in place. As it is not adjustable like the spring clip, however, the measurement of the 'leg' extension must match the measurement of extension of canvas beyond frame exactly.

A word of warning here: taping a stretcher on board into a frame without using nails is inadequate. However strong the tape may appear while new, it is perishable over a period of time or if subjected to the normal warmth of a household atmosphere. Tapes with a cloth base are liable to stretch so that a heavy picture could eventually pull away.

Screw eyes and similar attachments to carry the wire or cord are specially made for picture framing. Ordinary nails should not be used. The screws are fixed into the back of the frame, carefully positioned so that they are not visible from the front. If the screw is sunk well in until the ring is resting against the wood, there will be less strain on the thread part of the screw. Small screw eyes are firm enough for small to medium frames, so long as the picture is not heavy, but a larger and heavier picture needs a more substantial attachment.

The position of the screws should be in the

Step 9

Measure about one-third of the way down the frame from the top on each side and make pencil marks for the position of the screw eyes. Punch the holes with a bradawl to a depth slightly less than the thread of the screw, with the holes sloping upwards to give maximum security, and allow them to take the strain of weight. You may need to widen the top of each hole by twisting the bradawl round so that the screw will enter more easily.

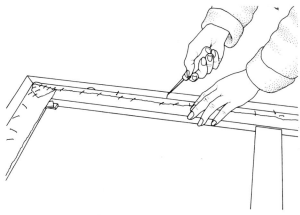

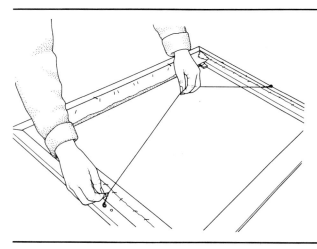

Step 10

Unravel the picture wire, push one end through the first screw eye to a length of several centimetres and pass it back through the eye again. Wind the end tightly round and round the wire, turn it and wind back towards the eye a little way, then tuck it under. Now pull the wire across and pass it through the other eye. With the other hand pull out enough of the wire to the correct tension but not enough to show above the top of the picture. Cut the wire, allowing the extra beyond the screw eye and wind it round as for the first side.

thickest part of the frame and not too close to either edge. Very thin moulding may split when a screw is inserted. In such cases, fix the hangers to the back of the stretcher, but they must be fixed securely to prevent them from pulling out of the soft wood.

If the back of the canvas is untidy, with ragged edges, loose threads can be trimmed away. Unless the linen and nails are visible from the sides when the picture is hung, there is no real need to tape over them.

Stranded picture wire is best for framing as it will last a long time and it will not stretch, whereas ordinary string will not last and will break easily. If you do use cord, make sure it is a good thick 'stranded' variety, such as blind cord which is quite tough and will neither break nor stretch.

Before hanging the painting, check the walls. Some walls, particularly outer ones, are concrete-backed and will not accept nails unless the wall is drilled, whereas interior walls are more likely to be receptive. Test the wall by tapping it: if there is a hollow sound, it will usually take a sharp picture nail. Insert the nail at a slight angle with the head sloping upwards to prevent the wire slipping off the top.

Right: The acrylic painting, Morning Walk near Benirama *by Melissa Lipkin, 1976, is shown here in its finished pine-wood frame hanging on a beige bedroom wall. Soft tones of yellow and brown are repeated in the dressing-table and chair, and the yellow and green plants echo similar colours in the picture.*

Project 2
Mounting a Water-Colour Behind Glass

A combination of frame, glass and mount (mat) is an ideal way of presenting a piece of art such as a water-colour, etching, drawing or pastel. The mount provides a transitional area or breathing space between picture and frame, and the glass protects the surface of both picture and mount, while the frame holds all the component pieces together. The small water-colour illustrated here is a typical example of the range of paper-based pictures which can be framed in this way.

The colour, width and design of both mount and frame as usual depends on the type and size of the picture. Choose the mount colour before deciding on the width, and before selecting the frame. This will make it easier to achieve a unified result.

A work containing several different colours needs a mount in a shade that will blend with all the colours without echoing any one too strongly. It is more difficult to decide on a mount colour when the picture tones are divided into separate sections as, for instance, in a landscape with a definite horizon line dividing sky from earth containing clumps of trees or buildings, where the respective colours are in strong contrast. In comparison, a small painting containing a blend of soft colours with similar tone and strength should have a mount which is neutral and bland, otherwise the picture will lose its subtlety.

This water-colour, although small, has fairly strong colouring which can take a mount of similar strength. The one chosen is a medium grey-green, neither too dark nor too light, the colour complementing the trees in the painting without being too heavy. Other colour samples of card tried against this landscape were: cream, which could be a natural choice but, in the event, proved too light and bland; olive green, which was too strong, made the water-colour altogether too heavy and green by over-emphasizing the greenness of the trees; blue-grey simply looked wrong, as the landscape contained little blue, except for a tiny bit of pale sky; beige colours, complementary to both red and green, were too warm as a surround.

Once the right mount has been chosen, it is time to consider the frame. The width of the mount can be decided at the same time as moulding samples are tried against mount card and picture. In most cases, the frame should be narrower than the mount to provide a harmonious contrast in width. A suitable type of moulding for a simple drawing or sketch would be a plain, thin shape, curved or rounded, but a more colourful pastel or water-colour can take a more complex shape. Small pictures with mounts usually need thinner and plainer frames, although a compromise for a small-to-medium size image could be a simple moulding with one or two ridges or a beaded inner edge.

Left: Some of the necessary component pieces and tools accompany the small water-colour before it is mounted and framed. The sheet of glass placed halfway over the mount card shows a slight colour difference which should be noted, especially when planning a subtle surround.

The colour of the frame must relate to both the mount shade and the picture. A wooden moulding, plain or coloured, may well complement either a drawing or a painting, and ready-made gilt or silver moulding can enhance the same type of artwork. Gilt blends well with paintings which have predominantly warm colours whereas silver tones with those which have predominantly cool shades. An ideal solution for a picture which has a mixture of cool and warm colours is to soften a silver frame with a rub of paint or lacquer to give it a silver-gilt tone.

Experiment with wood stains and paints on off-cuts of moulding to help decide the right shade for the particular artwork. Interesting results can be obtained by mixing stains together. This frame is a close-grained oak wood, light in colour. A mixture of rosewood stain and medium oak was chosen. The resultant colour echoes the red house in the picture and provides a pleasant contrast to the colour of the mount, without being alienated from it. An experiment with a plain oak stain resulted in a cool brown which was too dull for the reds in the picture, but mixing it with rosewood produced the desired shade of warmth. Other brown colours such as mahogany or walnut, although warm in tone, would be much too strong for such a painting.

First prepare the moulding lengths to remove any roughness in the wood, as described in Project 1. The moulding should be coloured after the frame is cut but before it is joined together, as it is then easier to apply the stain evenly. The shape of some mouldings makes it difficult to colour the corners of a made-up frame, often resulting in a messy 'build up' of colour in the corners, whereas the rest of the frame has a lighter and more even tone. If the made-up frame is a simple shape, however, like the one chosen to accentuate the little water-colour, it is possible to put the wood stain on evenly, but it must be applied liberally so that it reaches the small channels and crevices in the wood. It must also be applied fairly quickly, especially if the wood is porous, to ensure an even colour.

After application of the stain (or paint, if used) the moulding should be set aside to dry for at least half a day, depending on the temperature. Wood stains often dry to a lighter shade, so a second coat may be needed if a darker effect is required.

The size of the mount for the picture must be determined before the frame size can be finalized. With mount and picture together, the frame size is calculated, using the outer edge of the mount as the measurement, and adding an extra 2 mm ($\frac{1}{16}$ in) to length and width for ease of fitting. The frame can then be cut and joined following the instructions in Project 1, and after retouching it can be waxed and polished as necessary.

Work from the inner or picture edge to the outer or finished edge when planning the mount measurements. First decide on the width. The margin is normally approximately one-fifth of the picture size: small to medium pictures could take 5–8 cm (2–3 in) margins and larger ones 8–10 cm (3–4 in) or more.

Measure the picture from side to side to find the inner measurement for the mount, making an

Step 1

Apply the stain with a thick wad of cotton wool in one long, continuous sweep along the length of the wood. Allow time for the first coat to be absorbed, then repeat the operation in the opposite direction to ensure that all the grain of the wood has received the stain. If the moulding is too broad to span in one operation, two long sweeps will be needed.

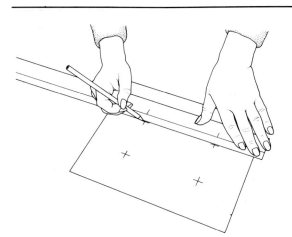

Step 2

With card face down on a clean, flat surface, mark off the grid for the opening of the mount: margin measurement, picture measurement, opposite margin measurement. Mark the same measurements further down the card at approximately the place the other side measurements will cross. Now turn the card around and mark the other side measurements in two places as before, crossing those marks already made. Join up the cross-marks to use as guides for cutting the mount and check for overall squareness, using a set square.

Step 3

Holding the steel ruler firmly along the line, insert the knife at an angle pointing slightly inwards and not more than 3 mm (⅛ in) outside the corner point. This allows for the bevel extension on the upper side of the mount which is not visible from the back. With the side of the knife resting against the rule to act as a support, draw the knife firmly and evenly down the line without stopping. Extend the cut very slightly beyond the corner-mark as at the beginning.

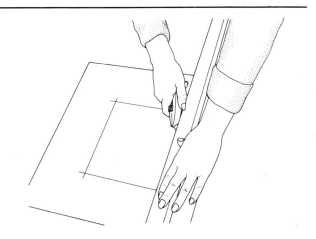

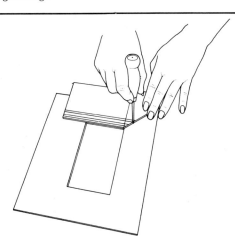

Step 4

Place the line and wash template on the mount, aligning it with the upper bevelled edge of the mount and the mitred corner. With a bradawl or pin gently mark off the various points for the lines and edges which will contain the wash section. Turn the mount around and plot for the remaining three corners.

Step 5

Using a lining pen with screw attachment adjusted to the right width of line, dip the pen into the prepared ink of water-colour mixture then wipe away any excess liquid. Take a ruler with an under-cut inner edge and align it on one side between the inner pin marks, so that the inner edge is raised away from the card. In this way blots are less likely to occur when drawing lines. Draw the inner line along from point to point on one side. Turn the card and repeat for the other three sides.

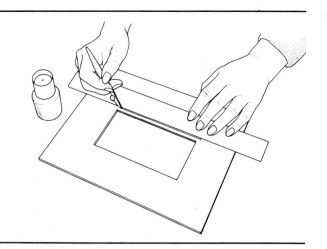

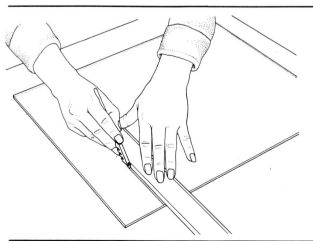

Step 6

Water lines have been drawn with the lining pen and ruler between the inner and outer points on one side. While these lines are still wet, dip the brush into the colour mixture, then draw it along between the two wet lines which will serve as a restraint and prevent the wash from seeping over. The width of the brush should cover the width of the wash. Repeat on the remaining three sides. It may be necessary to dip into the colour, keeping the wash even and liquid until all four sides have been covered.

Step 7

To fit the picture to the mount, cut a piece of masking tape the width of the picture, place the picture face down and attach the tape along the upper edge so that half the tape is overlapping. Turn the picture face up, lay the mount over it in the correct position and press down firmly over the taped area so that the one half of the tape is joined to the picture and the other half to the mount. Turn picture and mount face down, and attach another strip of tape to the bottom edge of the picture with half of it overlapping as before.

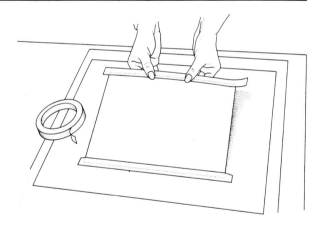

Step 8

Place the ruler on the sheet of glass about 2 mm (⅟₁₆in) away from the marked line to allow for the distance between the cutting wheel and the side of the ruler. Without stopping, draw the glass cutter along the line, keeping a firm and even pressure, but there is no need to press too hard. This will score the surface of the glass and it can be broken by bending it lightly over the edge of the table using a slight pressure.

Step 9

With a ruler and sharp knife, score firmly along the marked lines of the hardboard using heavy pressure. Bend the board back firmly and, if the knife has made enough impression, it will split. Run the knife along this section again if the board has not split right through, to cut away the excess completely. Smooth the rough edges of the board with either a rasp or sandpaper.

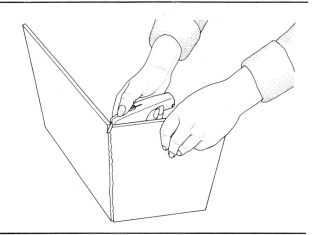

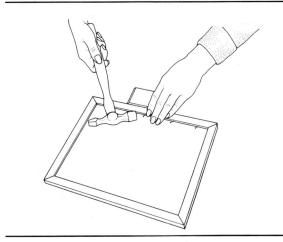

Step 10

To assemble the picture, place the frame face down and slip the glass, picture and board into it. Prick a hole with the bradawl held at a sloping angle and as flat as possible against the backing board. Insert a nail into the hole and keep it pressed flat with your first finger while supporting the outer edge of the frame with a wooden chock held in place by your thumb. Hammer the nail in at an angle until it is secure, but with enough of it protruding to keep the picture in place. Insert nails in the same way around the frame at intervals of 5 cm (2 in).

allowance for the overlap of the mount edge. A water-colour painting or pastel may have roughly-finished edges which make it out of square, so the measurements taken should be the minimum on each side to ensure that the rough edges will be covered by the mount. In this case, measure carefully across the painting in several places for each side.

Mounts can be cut from the front of the card with the knife sloping outwards, or from the back of the card with the knife sloping inwards. I always cut mounts from the back as I find it easier to control both the knife and the ruler to get a perfect bevelled edge. Also, the pencilled guide lines (Step 2) will not be visible on the back, whereas they will be from the front of the card. In this case, they will have to be removed later, not an easy job if they are on the sharp bevel, and an eraser may damage the surface of the card.

If you have not cut a mount before, practise on spare pieces of card. It takes time to learn to relax and achieve an even knife pressure. For a first attempt it is probably wise to choose a small picture to mount because more sustained concentration is necessary to cut a large mount, and even a slight wobbling of the knife can cause a wavy bevelled edge which will be very noticeable when the mount is fitted to the picture.

Measure and mark up the card as described in Step 2. Use a sharp knife for cutting and put a spare piece of card under the mount card to take the blade

in case it sinks through to the chipboard support. This also prevents the knife from becoming blunt quickly. Each blade should last for several mounts, depending on size. If blunt blades are used, the resulting bevel will not be clean and sharp. The width and slant of the bevel depends on the angle at which the knife is held. Check the edge of the steel ruler occasionally by running a finger along it to make sure there are no nicks in the steel, as these will make the blade jump slightly when it hits them and cause bumps in the bevelled edge of the card. Any small nicks or scratches can usually be removed by rubbing the length of the ruler with a lightly oiled piece of fine emery paper (sandpaper), then cleaning it carefully with a cloth.

Do not throw away the centre cut-out part from the mount card until you are sure that it cannot be used for a smaller mount. If the cutting has not extended far enough beyond the corners, the centre may not come away easily. To find the problem, carefully turn over the whole mount with the centre still attached. It may be that the knife has not penetrated a tiny portion of the upper layer of paper which could tear away if the mount is handled carelessly. Simply cut away this little piece with a sharp knife and the ruler, so that the centre comes away cleanly.

An alternative to using a sharp knife is the commercial mount-cutting tool into which the blade is screwed at an angle. The screw-section can be moved slightly to alter the angle of the blade. You will have to make an allowance of 3 mm ($\frac{1}{8}$ in) or so between the drawn lines and the side of the ruler, as the blade is not right up against the ruler (as it is when using a sharp knife) but slightly away from it.

Although small, some pictures such as this may need some sort of decorative addition to the mount to blend the inner edge of the mount with the painting. The use of soft colours in line/wash (Steps 5 and 6) repeated in the frame and picture, will help to bring mount, picture and frame together and make a small painting more distinctive. However, the margin must be wide enough to accommodate this effect without looking 'pinched'. The margin width here is 7 cm ($2\frac{3}{4}$ in) on top and sides and 7.5 cm (3 in) on the bottom. Some pictures are improved by adding an extra 6 mm ($\frac{1}{4}$ in) to the bottom margin as this helps the proportion of the mount in relation to the picture when it is hung. Large pictures could take an extra 13–20 mm ($\frac{1}{2}$–$\frac{3}{4}$ in) added to the bottom margin, but a small picture needs only a little.

The wash used here, about 6 mm ($\frac{1}{4}$ in) wide, is a greenish-grey, a slightly darker tone than that of the mount itself, but not too heavy because the picture is small and could easily be overpowered. The inner line is ochre, and the outer one a light Indian red. Coloured inks can be used for lines, and water-colours can be mixed and diluted for wash channels. Try several combinations of lines and wash on spare pieces of card of the same colour, as they tend to dry to a different tone from that when wet, then adjust them accordingly. For this picture and mount a white inner line (intending to pick up the fine white lines in the painting) does not work as it is not strong enough and is too close in tone to the colour of the mount; a pinkish-brown wash, although it could tie in well with the brown frame and the red in the picture, would make the overall effect too predominantly red-brown, alienating the greys and greens in mount and picture; yellow or blue lines or wash would look out of place, as there is not enough of these colours in the painting.

If you intend to repeat the same mount, perhaps for a series of similar pictures, it is a good idea to mix enough colour for several line/wash and store it in a small jar. As the colour pigment will eventually separate from the water it cannot be kept for too long. When diluted, inks tend to separate in the same way, producing a mottled result, which can be interesting, but it is difficult to control this effect during application. For a smooth wash it is therefore better to use water-colour. Small corner samples can be made up and kept, with a record of the colours used written on the reverse of the card.

To make a template for plotting the exact positions of the lines and wash, measure a corner section of card using a set square to make a perfect 45° angle running from the inner corner of the mount to the outer one, and cut it with a straight, not bevelled, edge. Determine the distance you need between the various lines and mark spots for them close to the angle-edge of the template. You can then match the exact positions for the lines as you plot them at each corner of the mount when the template is placed against it. The lines when joined will then run straight.

Recipes for variations of line and wash can be kept by making a series of points on the template, numbering them and, using the numbers, keeping a record of the combinations. For a wash, it may be necessary to record the proportion of parts mixed with water, especially if the wash consists of two or more colours mixed together.

The pin-marks are joined up with the lining pen as described in Step 5. Although the lines may be drawn in with pencil, it can show through a light wash and spoil an otherwise subtle effect. Manipulating the wash channel is more difficult than drawing the lines, as an even wash must be obtained. Hence, the wash should be applied with the brush fairly full, not dry, so that the liquid can be swirled around (if it appears to be uneven) by tilting the card in different directions.

If the atmosphere is warm or the mount large, the paint will obviously dry out more quickly, so keep an eye on the first corner and dab it lightly with water to prevent a hard edge forming across the channel as it dries out. Any slight discrepancies in the wash can usually be removed by softly scraping the area with a moistened bristle brush after the paint has dried.

The mount must be set aside to dry on a flat surface, otherwise the wash will dry out unevenly. Wavy edges of the wash can be straightened by adding a line of the same colour and tone to 'draw' the edge together, but this must be done after the wash has dried. The width of the lines can be altered from thin to thick by adjusting the screw on the lining pen.

This particular water-colour was attached to the mount with masking tape (Step 7). Other types of tapes such as resin-based adhesives are unsuitable, as the tape can contract with age and make the picture buckle. The resin also leaves a brown stain on the paper which is very difficult to remove without damaging the picture. If the painting is valuable, or the paper is particularly delicate, stamp hinges can be used, one attached to each top corner. The glass at the front and the firm backing will keep the picture flat. When taping the picture into the mount, take care not to pull the paper taut or the mount will buckle after it is fitted into the frame, and if the paper is thin it may split.

Glass is necessary for sealing both the picture and the mount into the frame and protecting them from dust and dirt. As with mount-cutting, you should practise glass-cutting on small pieces of spare glass to become familiar with the cutter, learning to use it with ease and precision. Glass must be handled with great care, and off-cuts should be removed and stored somewhere out of the way.

To measure the glass before cutting, place one corner of the piece tight into the made-up frame and mark it with a felt tip (fibre) pen. The measurement should be 2 mm ($\frac{1}{16}$ in) less than the rebate (rabbet) measurement to allow for easy fitting in the same way as the mount. Now swing the glass around and mark the other side, then join up the marks as guide-lines. Take the glass from the frame and place it on the bench for cutting, with a firm, soft backing such as thick cotton or felt.

Left: The water-colour by Marie-Louise Avery, now mounted and with a reddish-brown stained frame. The line and wash on the mount provides a link with the greens in the picture while the frame colour blends with the red of the house. The neutral colour of the wall makes a satisfying background, and the trees in the picture are highlighted by the plant in the foreground.

The ordinary glass-cutting tool which scores the surface rather than actually cutting into it is quite adequate for thin picture glass. A wooden stay-piece may be used as a guide instead of a metal ruler, but it must be straight and smooth.

Draw the cutting wheel along so that it extends over both top and bottom edges. Do not work over the same cutting line twice as this will destroy the sharp edges of the scored line and make the glass break unevenly. It may also damage the wheel of the cutting tool. Before each cutting motion dip the wheel into turpentine to keep it oiled for smooth travel across the glass.

Another method of breaking glass from the one described in Step 8 is to hold the glass with one hand on each side of the cut-mark, thumbs uppermost, then gently press the fingers upwards from underneath so that the glass splits. If the glass does not break cleanly and small pieces remain sticking out, these can be chipped away very carefully with the teeth on the cutter, although it is difficult to break such small sections away without breaking the piece of glass in another direction.

Dust the work surface very carefully to sweep up any tiny shreds of glass. Although such splinters may be practically invisible, they can easily be picked up on your hands and become embedded in the skin.

Hardboard (masonite) makes ideal backing board as it combines firmness with lightness and durability, and is available in several thicknesses, the thinner type being appropriate for a small picture. Cardboard is not suitable as it is too thin and may warp, and it will not withstand moisture or insect attack. The backing board must be the same size as the mount or glass. As it will be placed with the rough side facing inwards, an interleaving piece of thick paper or thin conservation card should be inserted as a protection for the back of the painting.

Dust all the component parts before fitting the picture into the frame. Remove finger-marks from the mount with a soft eraser, splinters of wood from the inside rebated edge of the frame and chips from the edges of the backing board. Clean the glass, using a lint-free cloth, with methylated spirits which evaporates, polishes up well, and leaves no smear-marks on the glass. Cleaning glass with water is tedious since it tends to leave smear-marks and it dries very slowly.

While nailing the picture into the frame, glance at the front to make sure that there are no flecks of dust or tiny chips of wood trapped between glass and picture; the hammering action often dislodges particles of dust and these will be magnified by the glass. They can be removed by inserting a long feather between glass and picture, sometimes combined with tapping the picture lightly.

The picture must be airtight so that dust cannot enter around the rebated edges after it is nailed in. Gummed brown paper, available in several widths is useful for this purpose as it will not detach easily once glued down. Masking tape could be used but it may lose its adhesion over a period of time and fall away in a warm room temperature.

Cut four strips of gummed paper, wide enough to cover the nails and reach the outer edge of the frame, and slightly longer than the sides of the frame. Run a damp sponge along one piece and press it firmly onto the back of the frame, aligning one edge first to the edge of the frame, then pressing inwards so that the paper covers the nails and sticks firmly to the backing board. Repeat for the other three sides of the frame, and cut away the excess at the corners with a sharp knife.

After attaching screw eyes and wire to the back of the frame as described in Project 1, the picture is ready for hanging.

Project 3
Block-Mounting
a Poster

Most people possess one or two colourful and eye-catching reproductions which are worthy of display, but not in a conventional frame. Such nostalgic items as travel posters, 'classic' advertisements, playbills or decorative posters from art exhibitions like the ones shown here, can be displayed simply without a frame or glass, by being glued onto a thick board, the edges coloured to give a neat finish, and the surface sprayed with fixative for protection.

First examine the paper to make sure it is suitable for gluing. Bear in mind that any paper-based work such as a signed artist's print will lose its value by being glued down onto a support. Prints sold in art shops are normally made of fairly strong and durable paper which can be pasted down satisfactorily so long as the job is done carefully and the paper is not subjected to uneven amounts of moisture and glue during the process. Very thin or shiny paper may react badly to moisture and form wrinkles which will be hard to control while laying down. Paper in this state may be better stuck to a thick card support, using a spray-pack type of adhesive.

Paper that has been treated carelessly, or left rolled up for some time, may have severe creases, and its fibres may have been stretched to such an extent that they have broken. Such creases will not flatten out entirely, and may be more noticeable when the print is glued onto an even, flat surface, especially if the surface has a shiny instead of a matt finish. You must decide whether or not the work is attractive enough to overcome any imperfections in this method of display.

The type and thickness of the board should next be considered. Hardware shops or wood merchants will readily cut board to a specific size while you wait. It is useful and cheaper to know how to cut it yourself, however, as there are sometimes off-cuts around the house which could be cut down to fit a picture.

Of the various types of board available, chipboard and hardboard (masonite) are the most commonly used for displaying artwork. Chipboard is normally obtainable in at least two thicknesses, 15 mm ($\frac{5}{8}$ in) and 20 mm ($\frac{3}{4}$ in), and hardboard 3 mm ($\frac{1}{8}$ in) and 6 mm ($\frac{1}{4}$ in). Although even thinner boards are also available, they tend to warp after a time and if subjected to warm atmosphere. Hardboard should not be used for larger works as it may warp, and the result will be disappointing if the finished picture does not hang flat against the wall. It is, however, quite suitable for a smaller print of, say, 30 x 25 cm (12 x 10 in). Chipboard can be used for pictures of any size, as a thick board gives a pleasant chunky backing to a very small print, and it will not warp even on a large scale.

Left: A typical range of decorative posters and prints suitable for hanging by the plastic strip method, but more permanently preserved by gluing onto board. Some have their own margins or lined surrounds which provide a neat finish around the edges, but the coloured edges of the board will supply this in any case. The Burne-Jones poster was chosen for this project.

Although in the method described here the poster is glued down with its edges right to the edges of the board, there are equally successful alternative ways of presentation. The board can be cut slightly larger than the picture, leaving a margin surround of board which can either be left in its natural state (if pale straw, earthy brown or grey colours are suitable) or painted, perhaps repeating a colour in the print. A more advanced method of display is to glue the picture onto board as described here, then attach this board to another larger one, which will give a margin to the picture and also a raised, platform effect. This provides an impressive setting, especially for a small, brightly-coloured print which is strong enough not to be threatened by a large surround. For a more exaggerated platform effect, small pieces of polystyrene or blocks of wood can be glued between the two boards, but hidden from sight, thus providing a gap and giving a rather unusual 'floating' appearance.

For a first attempt it might be wise to choose a small print, as it is naturally easier to deal with a smaller piece of paper than a larger, unwieldy one, especially if you are doing the job on your own. It is easier for two people to deal with a larger print, one person holding one end of it steady while the other guides it into place on the board.

Measure the poster across from edge to edge for width and depth. After the backing board has been cut, it should fit the print exactly. If the board is even slightly larger than the poster when they are fitted, it will give an untidy finish to the work, and it would be impractical to trim the board after the paper is laid down. If in doubt as to accuracy make the measurements a little smaller, as a hairsbreadth can easily be trimmed from the poster before it is glued down so that it fits exactly. Also, if you are dealing with a large poster, such as the one illustrated here, it may be awkward to place it on a sticky board with all four edges aligned perfectly. In this case, if the board is smaller, any overlapping edges of the paper can be trimmed away with a sharp blade and ruler after the paper has been glued down.

Cutting the board, as described in Step 1, should present little difficulty except that of keeping a larger board firmly in place during the sawing. In this case, it is a good idea to fix the main part of the board to the bench with a 'G' clamp (or two, one at each end, if possible). Use a panel saw as the tenon saw has a small, lipped section attached to the upper edge which prevents the freedom of movement necessary for a downward-sloping thrust.

To smooth the surface of the cut board, use a circular motion with a medium-weight sandpaper. This should remove any roughness in the pressed-chip layer of board, and any grease or shiny patches which would prevent good adhesion. Hardboard usually has a tough, shiny finish consisting of a compressed linseed oil film, and unless this is sanded away, paper may not adhere to the surface permanently as there is not enough 'tooth' to give a firm grip, so that the poster will lift away from the board after six months or so. This is more likely to occur if a smooth glue such as PVA is used, rather

Step 1

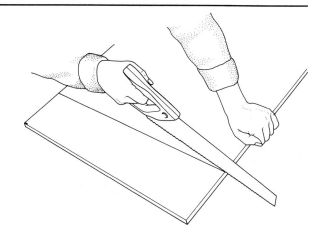

The measurements for the outer edges of the poster are clearly marked in pencil on a piece of chipboard. Lay the board on a firm surface, with the section which is to be cut away projecting over the edge. With one hand holding the board in position, saw along the marked lines, using an even, forward thrust.

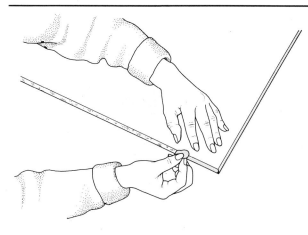

Step 2

Sand the edges of the board to remove excess chips and soften the sharp edges. Brush PVA glue along the sides into the crevices. Make little knobs of wood filler and use to build up any cracks by rubbing it along the rough sides and pressing firmly into the crevices. Work on small areas at a time as the filler dries out quickly. Wipe away the excess filler with your fingers as you go along.

Step 3

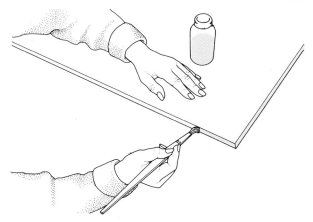

When the wood filler has dried and been sanded to a smooth surface, coat the edges with acrylic paint to match colours in the poster being laid down. Use a lining fitch brush of between 13–20 mm (½–¾ in) wide, keeping the V-shape of the brush at a slight angle as you paint along the edge. It does not matter if a little paint spills over onto the front, as the poster will be glued right up to the edges, thus covering any paint overflow. Put the paint on fairly thickly as the wood filler may be porous.

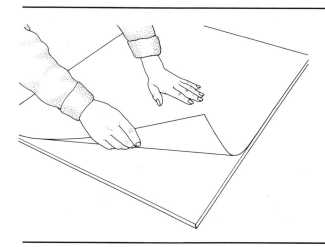

Step 4

After applying glue evenly to the board, position the poster on it. Lay the paper carefully, aligning the top and one side first, then gradually continue downwards, using one hand to smooth the paper gently, while the other guides the rest into position. Keep the edges of the paper aligned with the board, otherwise the picture will be crooked when you reach the bottom. If the glue is thick enough and tacky it is usually possible to adjust the position.

Step 5

At this stage, it is important to get rid of any air trapped under the paper. Flatten the poster and remove air pockets by working from the centre outwards with hands held flat, using a light pressure and circular motion. Sensitive fingers are best initially to find and flatten air-bubbles and lumps. A soft padding of cloth can then be used for an all-over flattening, but avoid rubbing too hard or the distribution of glue will be uneven as it is forced from one area to another.

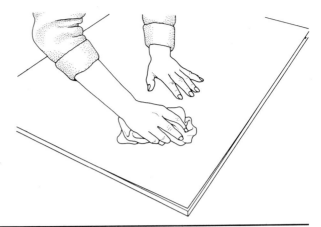

Step 6

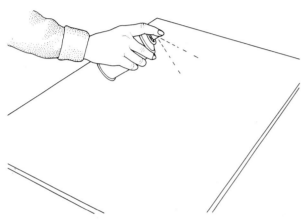

When the glue is thoroughly dried, spray the poster with varnish to give it a protective surface. Place the board face up on a background of newspaper. Shake the can well, hold it about 15–20 cm (6–8 in) away from the poster at a 45° angle and spray evenly backwards and forwards from side to side and over all the edges so that the whole area is covered.

Step 7

On the back of the board measure about a third down from the top and about a quarter of the width in from each side, and mark off with criss-cross lines. Bend each glass plate at the ringed section by pressing it downwards on the edge of the table (so that the wire can be slipped through the holes easily). Place the glass plates on the marked lines at a slight angle pointing upwards and mark the screwholes with a bradawl, then insert the screws with a screwdriver.

than an epoxy resin adhesive. It is therefore wiser to use the latter type of adhesive if you have a board with a semi-shiny surface. PVA is a suitable adhesive for the poster illustrated in this project, however, as the chipboard is not shiny.

After the board has been dusted to remove all gritty particles caused by sanding, the surface can be checked for irregularities by holding it up against the light at a slight angle.

The edges of some types of board, especially coarse chipboard, are particularly rough. These sides must be sanded and filled as in Step 2 to remove any loose chips which may otherwise break away later. The edges of hardboard can be ground down first with a rasp, then sanded. Fill in any large irregularities using a palette knife or spatula with either a ready-made filler or whiting mixed with PVA glue on a piece of glass or board.

Pay as much attention to the colour of the edges as to any other detail. The colours most frequently seen on edges are natural, white or black. An oak wood-filler will provide the natural colour similar to that of chipboard, which does not need painting and can be waxed lightly for protection. Black edges are suitable for a print or poster which has a hint of black running through the design, but a striking effect can be achieved by using any other colour which appears in the picture. The Burne-Jones poster has predominantly red and brown colouring and, in this case, a dull medium tone of Indian red was chosen to

Left: The Burne-Jones poster glued onto chipboard is shown against a brick background, the soft red and brown tones complementing the colours of the picture. The soft light is in keeping with the rough background and medieval subject matter.

reflect the brownish-reds in the design. The brighter red which also appears in the design would be too strong as an edge colour. It may be necessary, as here, to mix two or more colours to achieve the exact shade.

It is probably easier to paint the edges before the paper is laid onto the board (Step 3). Although the edges can be painted after the print is glued and dried, it is slow and tedious as you have to keep wiping spilt paint from the surface of the print, especially if using a quick-drying paint such as acrylic.

Damping the board well with water will provide a receptive ground for the glue and prevent if from drying out too quickly. Most pressed-fibre boards are porous and the water will sink in as it is applied. In some cases it is necessary to wet the back of the paper too, especially if it is thick and porous, before laying it down.

When the poster is put on the board, work out of a draught if possible, as even the smallest particles of dust trapped under the paper will be noticeable. If you are using PVA adhesive it may need to be diluted a little with water to make it a spreadable consistency. It should be put on fairly generously and broadly, then brushed out to an even film. A spatula or palette knife is useful to help spread the glue quickly over a large area. You can pick any small lumps from the sticky surface as they appear. After the paper has been laid down, any glue seeping out around the edges should be removed with a damp cloth before it dries.

The use of clear varnish applied to the paper is optional, but it will certainly protect the picture from dust, grime or flyspots and give it a longer life, as a piece of glass would. Also the surface can be cleaned with a damp cloth whenever necessary. Either matt or gloss varnish can be used, depending upon the surface desired. The spray-pack finish is easily obtainable, the most convenient to apply (Step 6), and dries within minutes. The other alternative is to brush on a ready-made paper varnish, but it is less easy to get an even overall result.

Once the face of the picture has dried, it is time to attach the hangers to the back. The choice of fixture and length of screws depends on the thickness of the board. A thick chipboard will take screws between 6 and 13 mm ($\frac{1}{4}$ and $\frac{1}{2}$ in). The screws must obviously be shorter than the width of the board or they will go through to the front. Thinner hardboard will not take screws, and shorter ones will be insecure for hanging the picture. If the picture is on hardboard, 'D' rings can be attached to small squares of similar board with rivets, then the small squares can be glued to the back of the picture on each side and placed under weights until dry.

The most convenient hanging fixture for this poster on chipboard is the glass plate which has two screw-holes and another hole to carry the hanging wire. The glass plates are attached to the back of the board as described in Step 7, after which the wire can be threaded through and the picture is then ready for hanging.

Project 4
Leather Frame
for a Photograph

The availability of reasonably priced and portable photographic equipment of good quality enables the enterprising amateur to produce photographs of a high standard which can be regarded as pictures in their own right. Colour photographs of memorable holiday scenes, family occasions and portraits of friends, or monochrome mood shots of buildings or landscapes, are all capable of being taken out of the album and into the drawing-room. Similarly, a growing interest in old photographs which provide a fascinating insight into the lives of previous generations, has caused many people to dust down examples for display in a room setting.

Many photographs are on a much smaller scale than paintings or prints, and the details of the composition – whether portrait, figures or landscape – are consequently finer. The framing should therefore be kept as simple as possible. However, with less detailed photographs or those that have been 'blown up' to a larger scale, it is possible to use bolder, brighter colouring and design.

If the photograph is small, the frame chosen might be small also, but of a contrasting colour to the mount (mat). Many people, however, prefer to have a wider, thicker frame on a small photograph, combined with a very narrow mount or no mount at all. An older photograph presented in this way can look attractive with a rich, dark wood stain on the moulding, especially if it is sepia-tinted.

A series of small photographs can form a satisfying group when displayed together in one mount with several openings and within the one frame. In this case, the juxtaposition and measurements between the photographs must be planned with care.

Black and white photographs should be treated carefully, as too vivid or contrasting colours, for instance, will only make them look drab. A simple grey or buff of the appropriate tone, or white, is often all that monochrome photographs need in the way of a mount. Colour photographs, whether bright or subdued, can be treated in much the same way as other artwork: by choosing mount and frame colours which are either repeated from the picture or compatible with it.

The framing described here combines an oval-centred mount with glass and a frame covered in leather. It has a strut back (easel back), also leather-covered, so that the finished picture can stand on a shelf or table-top as an alternative to hanging.

The small sepia photograph has a horizontal oval opening and its own rectangular surround. A few obvious colours for the mount would be light off-white, pale mushroom or dark sepia. However, a medium tone of dull gold was chosen as the paler colours are too light for the brownish tones in the picture and this, although more of a contrast, is still harmonious with the warm sepia. This mount was

Left: Leather, mount and glass for framing the small oval photograph. The leather-covered frame is seen from the reverse, showing the edges tucked under and glued neatly into place. The gold mount has not yet been attached to the photograph.

bought ready-cut as it is difficult to cut an accurate oval or circular mount and much good card can be wasted by trying.

If you want to try cutting your own oval or circular mount, pottery dishes and bowls may provide useful templates for the right shape and size. Alternatively, experiment with a piece of string tied in a loop placed around two nails fixed into the card: many different shapes can be made by drawing with a pencil held against the taut string. Use a compass to form a circle. Cutting the mount freehand is simplified by nailing the piece of card to the bench through the central part which will be cut away. This will prevent the card from slipping about as you swing the card around slowly with one hand while cutting along the drawn line with the other.

Of the many types of material suitable for gluing onto a wooden frame, leather, suede, linen, thick silk or velvet are probably the most commonly used. In many cases, simulated fabrics, provided they are of good quality, will do just as well for framing. Texture, as well as colour, is obviously an important consideration. For a fine photograph such as this one, a smooth finish is desirable, as any fabric with a pronounced weave, such as linen, would look too coarse when placed against the image.

For this small photograph, leather of a medium tan brown was chosen, a colour which blends well with the gold mount and the sepia tones of the picture. Setting this leather on the chubby shaped moulding with mitred corners gives a hand-crafted, old-world effect which is appropriate to the subject matter.

A relatively wide moulding – 2.5 cm (1 in) used here – with several ridges gives a more interesting result than a plain flat or rounded shape, but remember that it is harder to glue fabric successfully onto a moulding of exaggerated proportions than onto one that is plain. For a successful combination, decide on the type of material at the same time as the type and shape of moulding.

It is not easy to manipulate too thin a fabric as it may pull about alarmingly and the glue can seep through leaving a stain which will probably be irremovable. In the same way, liquid glue will come through a coarse cloth with an open weave unless a latex rubber-based adhesive is used. Hides are fairly easy to deal with because of their suppleness. Their synthetic counterparts are also supple, and the manufacturers often provide instructions concerning their adhesives.

The amount of material needed depends on how it is applied to the frame: it can be cut into mitred strips and applied to the four sides of the frame, or the whole rectangle can be cut out and applied to the frame in one piece. If there is only a limited amount of material obviously the first method will be the most convenient. Different colours of the same fabric can be cut into sections and glued onto the moulding side by side in a variety of patterns to achieve an interesting effect. If the second method is used, there will be difficulty making a woven fabric follow the shape of a moulding which has a pronounced contour or sharp ridges, especially at the corners.

Step 1

Place the photograph face down on a clean, dry surface. Cut a piece of masking tape 13 mm (½ in) or wider and long enough to overlap the edges of the photograph. Stick the tape along the upper edge of the photograph with half overlapping. Turn the photograph face up, and lower the oval mount onto it, then press firmly together over the part where the tape will grip to the under-side of the mount. Turn it over and press down to make sure the tape has stuck.

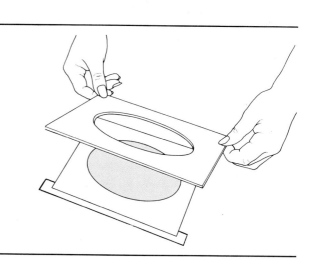

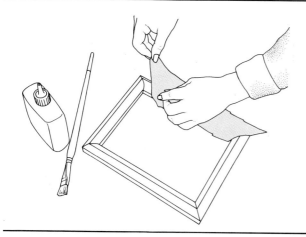

Step 2

Apply PVA glue fairly liberally to one side of the made-up frame and also to the wrong side of a strip of leather already cut to size. Work on one side at a time as the glue may dry out quickly. While the glue is still tacky, place the leather strip over the frame, lining up the corners, and press down on the front, gradually working over the sides, but leaving the underneath, back and rebate, until later. Repeat with the other three sides, being careful that the leather mitred corners meet, easing them together so that they overlap a little, if necessary.

Step 3

When the leather has dried enough not to move around when touched, turn the frame over and run a little glue around the inside rebate edges. Press the overlap of leather gently into position, making sure that it is not too wide and does not extend beyond the rebate width. If it does, trim off the excess before gluing down. Trim the outer edges of the leather in the same way and glue them down also. It may be necessary to cut away small V-shapes at the corners to avoid too much bulk there.

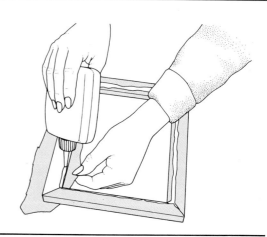

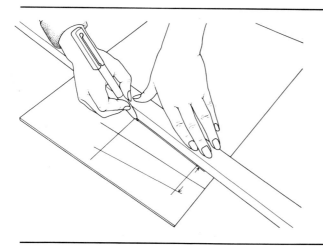

Step 4

To make a strut for a free-standing frame, first work out the length of strut in relation to size of frame. Next, draw a straight vertical line on a piece of stiff card to the right length and rule horizontal lines across at top and bottom. As the top of the strut must be slightly narrower than the bottom, plot the points of the four outer corners by marking the exact measurements outwards from the central vertical line. Now join the top and bottom corners. Cut out the card strut with a sharp knife and glue leather pieces of the same shape and size to each side.

For a plain, flat moulding as used for a slip or inner frame, a firm non-stretch material, such as linen can be glued on one strip at a time down each side and the mitres cut afterwards. This makes for a neat finish so long as the corners are cut carefully with a very sharp knife and ruler lined up at the exact 45° angle. With this method the glue must be applied to the moulding only (*not* to the fabric), brushed on as far as the angle-line for each side, and as each strip is glued on it will overlap the corners of the one before.

Materials such as the thinner and better types of hide, however, are pliable in any direction and can consequently be eased into shape. Whichever method of application is adopted, the frame must first be made up, as sawing it after the fabric is laid would certainly result in bad fraying at the mitred edges. However, the very nature of leather means that some areas of the hide will be thinner or thicker than others. This is one good reason why the 'strip' method rather than the rectangular cut-out is to be preferred for such materials. Even so it is necessary to plot the strips so that they will be fairly consistent in thickness.

Measure and cut the strips very carefully. The material has to cover the side and front of the frame and extend under the rebate (rabbet) to the back of the moulding, with an overlap of at least 6 mm ($\frac{1}{4}$ in) in each case. Most frames will need a strip roughly twice their width, and extra must be allowed for deep ridges or prominent parts. The angles of the mitred corners must be exact and running true with those of the frame. You can work these out by plotting the inner and outer points of the frame and joining them together in a line, or by using a protractor. To simplify cutting the strips and to make sure they are the same, it is a good idea to make up a card template. Put this on the reverse side of the material, and mark out the strips by tracing around the template with a soft pencil or a felt tip (fibre) pen if the fabric is thick.

Fabric such as leather may stretch when wet with glue, and contract again after it is dry, which could result in 'split' mitred corners. In such cases, it is wise to cut the strips just a shade bigger, especially along the mitres. In the case of a chunky leather frame such as the one here, a slight overlap on the mitred corners is not offensive but merely adds to the hand-hewn look, and it is preferable to having gaps if the pieces do not quite meet.

Thinner fabric can be cut easily with scissors, but for leather or suede a very sharp blade is essential and a heavy steel ruler is needed for a firm grip on the material. When dealing with leather or a similar fabric which has a 'nap' backing, the mitre edge of the material should be clean-cut and sharp. If the blade is held at a slight angle while cutting this section, the furry texture of the inner side of the leather will not be so visible and cannot 'feather' out after the material is glued down.

Instant or very quick-drying glues are most unsatisfactory for this job, as they do not allow enough time to manipulate the fabric and position it correctly. For this reason it is again easier to deal with 'strips' which are applied one by one (see Step

2) rather than an overall rectangle. If the frame is large, however, it may be necessary to dilute the glue a little to prevent it from drying out too quickly. This will also give time to ease the fabric into recessed areas of the moulding. Wood-worker's glue (PVA), although fairly liquid, is ideal for thicker fabric such as velvet, leather or suede, and in fact, any material where the glue cannot soak through.

When working with a single piece of material the measurements must be exact because the material cannot be so easily adjusted if it is even a hairs-breadth out, as can the strips. Place the material face down with the frame face down on top, then roughly mark out the whole section with a soft pencil (remembering to allow for overlaps). Draw up the shape with a ruler and check carefully with a set square to make sure it is not crooked. Positioning the rectangle on the frame can be difficult, especially if the fabric is soft or pulls this way and that. Lower it gently over the frame, and adjust the whole piece while it can still be moved before pressing it firmly into place.

For a free-standing frame, the supporting strut must be sturdy and centrally positioned. It is attached to the backing board by means of a small hinged clip and bar. This attachment allows the strut movement so that the angle at which the picture stands can be adjusted.

The width of the strut varies according to the size of the picture and consequently the amount of weight it has to support. For a small frame, as here, it should normally be about 7–8 cm (3 in) wide at the bottom to ensure stability, perhaps tapering up to 5 cm (2 in) at the top – or at least wide enough to take the hinged clip attachment. The length of the strut should be roughly two-thirds of the height of the frame, and it should be attached about one-third from the top to make sure it will tilt at the right angle. You can judge the correct angle by standing the frame up, tilting it backwards until the angle is reached, then measuring the distance from one-third down on the frame to the surface of the table. As the strut must be at least 3 mm ($\frac{1}{8}$ in) thick so that it will not bend, use either a thin board or thick card.

For a neat finish, the backing board and both sides of the strut should be covered in the same material as the frame, because the back of a free-standing frame will be visible from different angles. The leather covering for the 'overall' backing illustrated here has an overlap of material which is tucked in and glued down on the inside of the board. The backing board should therefore be cut 3 mm ($\frac{1}{8}$ in) smaller to allow for the fabric folded over the edges so that the board does not end up being a little larger than the frame itself. Cover the strut in the same way, but cut the material for the *inner* side slightly smaller than the strut itself. When it is glued into place the ragged overlap will be hidden underneath.

When putting the strut on the frame just join the flap part of the attachment, after which the 'bar' section can be joined to the backing board. The rivets must be long enough to go through the board and fold over firmly for a secure grip. Position the flap on the *inside* of the strut and align it exactly

Step 5

The flap part of the hinge attachment has been joined to the strut with two rivets, lightly tapped on the inner side of the strut with a hammer. Place the strut on the leather-covered backing board in a central position and line up the base with the bottom of the frame, then mark the points through the small holes where the rivets will go to attach the other part of the hinge to the backing board. Check with a ruler to ensure that the strut is in a central position.

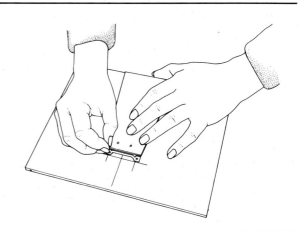

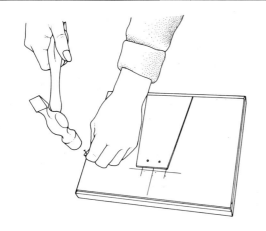

Step 6

Place the backing onto the frame and level up all the edges. Prick holes at intervals of 5 cm (2 in) or so around the edges of the board so that the nails will be in the thicker part of the frame, a little inwards from the edge of it. Now hammer the small brass pins, held straight, through the leather, the backing and into the frame so that the heads are flush with the surface of the board.

with the edge. The holes for the rivets can then be marked and punched with a bradawl, and the rivets inserted from the outside to the inside and tapped into place.

Because this is an overall backing and consequently is not holding the glass, mount and picture in position, find out if there is a space between the mounted photograph and the backing board. If there is, the space should be padded out with an extra piece of card to ensure that all the inner components will be held firmly in position. Otherwise the picture and the glass can flop backwards and forwards, especially when the frame is standing at an angle and it is moved about on a table or shelf.

When attaching the backing, it is a good idea to punch four holes – one near each corner – and hammer the nails into these, rather than working around one side of the frame at a time. There will then be less likelihood of the back slipping and ending up crooked. The remaining holes can then be punched and the nails hammered home.

Punch the holes with a really sharp bradawl because the hammering action should be kept to a minimum, as it might jar the glass and possibly cause it to break. If the backing material is thick, it may be difficult to punch holes through and into the frame in one operation, at the same time keeping control of the position. In this case, it is sensible to punch all the holes separately in the backing first, then place it onto the frame and punch through the holes into the moulding.

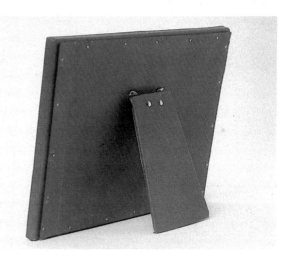

Above: The finished photograph frame seen from the reverse, showing the leather-covered strut back hinged onto the leather-covered backing board. The backing board is a hairsbreadth smaller than the back of the frame, and is attached with small brass pins.

Right: The Edwardian sepia photograph in gold mount and leather-covered frame is quite at home among the period clutter of the surrounding objects. The double, folding Victorian photograph frame is similar in colour and feeling, as are the two oval photographs.

Project 5
Antiqued Frame
for a Map

Many old printed or hand-coloured maps and other types of paper-based work are best displayed framed under glass but without a mount (mat). The antique quality of the paper is often charming and adds to the overall appeal of the work, while the margins outside the actual picture area give the necessary space which a mount would normally provide.

Like many prints and drawings which have lain rolled or folded and neglected over the years, the map illustrated here is torn and creased. It needs to be flattened out and repaired, put on a sheet of conservation board, and given an appropriately antiqued finish frame.

It is a matter of choice whether you trim the paper or not. If the outer edges are particularly rough and torn a little all the way round, a small sliver can be cut away, although in the case of valuable artwork trimming is always detrimental. If you must make the margin smaller, carefully fold back the edges, with a minimal amount of creasing which could damage the paper. The edges can always be ironed out at a later date but obviously cannot be put back once trimmed. I have seen old prints which have been whittled down, probably to make them fit easily into a made-up or readily available frame. These may have been trimmed gradually over the years, but the result is the same: the outer edge is cut away to within 13 mm ($\frac{1}{2}$ in) or so of the plate-mark or edge of the picture, where the margin would originally have been between 4 cm ($1\frac{1}{2}$ in) and 8 cm (3 in).

Remember that the rebate (rabbet), depending on its width, of the frame will cover up to 6 mm ($\frac{1}{4}$ in) or so of the edges. If, however, you want to show all the edges, the picture can be attached lightly to a piece of conservation board which has been cut slightly larger on all sides, thus ensuring that the edges are not covered.

Genuine antique prints, especially maps, are sometimes difficult to distinguish from those that are not so old (even, in some cases, newly printed) which have been treated to make them appear antique. Various methods are employed to achieve this effect, from a general 'distressing' to a more careful bathing in a fluid such as diluted tea to give the paper an authentic brown-with-age look.

Old prints, maps and other paper-based works which have been stored unframed, whether in a folder or not, have probably been fingered and have picked up slight marks and dust. Such paper should be given a careful surface clean, not with water, but with a soft eraser, preferably the 'kneadable' type which is less likely to scour the paper. Thin or delicate paper should be treated gingerly, especially

those areas which are creased and have loose fibres that could tear away. Areas with fine pencil work or faded water-colour, not easy to distinguish on an old picture, must be avoided.

You may find that genuinely old paper-work has been mended at some time. If the repair is recent it will be difficult to tell whether it is well done or not. Holes or tears will have patches of similar paper attached to the back. Should any tears remain it is best to flatten the whole picture first and then carry out the repair work. One or more isolated tears can then be mended and placed under weights individually without jeopardizing the overall flatness of the picture.

The easiest and most straight-forward way to flatten paper is described in Steps 1 and 2. Always remember to test the picture first to make sure that such media as ink or water-colour will not be affected by water. Certain types of ink may run when dampened, in which case the picture should be flattened using the ironing method only.

If you have a large heavy stack of paper or backing card, this can be used to flatten the art work instead of glass and weights. Slip the damp picture in between the pieces of card so that there is more weight on top than underneath and leave it to dry out. Blotting paper should be interleaved to protect the card from damp.

Badly damaged and creased paper may not flatten out satisfactorily by this method alone. If the paper has a plate-mark from the printing press, ripples often develop during the weighting and drying process. With care, these can be ironed out. The buckling which formed on the map used here was due to the already patched strip running down the centre, in that the paper on either side was buckled in the first place, and the weighting simply emphasized the wrinkles.

Use a warm iron only as the paper, depending on its thickness, could also buckle under intense heat. A bad wrinkle should be dampened lightly and a piece of blotting paper inserted between the iron and the picture. If the result is still unsatisfactory, this process can be repeated. Do not exert hard pressure or hold the iron in any one place for more than a few seconds at a time, as there is always the risk of scorching the paper. It is not easy to ascertain how a particular degree of temperature will affect a particular type of paper, and it is always wiser to be on the safe side.

Thicker, stronger types of paper may be smoothed out by 'straining'. The dampened paper is attached by masking tape on all four sides to a level rigid support. As the paper dries out it will contract and flatten, but is kept in position by the tape. Fragile paper would undoubtedly split under such strain. If necessary, the water can be applied to the back of the paper, which makes this method suitable for those pictures whose ink or colour may run. The paper must not be too damp or it will not accept the tape. One edge is attached to the board, then the opposite edge is attached, stretching the paper only very slightly, and the other two sides are treated in the same way. A word of caution: do not

Left: This nineteenth-century map of Spain does not look very badly damaged at first glance. Closer inspection reveals that it is buckled, with a strong central crease from being folded at some time, and there are small tears at the edges. The paper needs flattening to remove curled edges and creases, a surface cleaning to remove smudges and the tears repaired with mulberry paper and flour and water paste.

Step 1

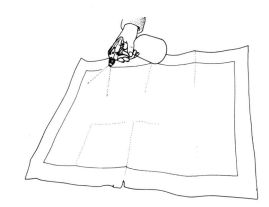

Place the map on a flat surface with a backing of blotting paper. Spray with an atomizer containing distilled water until the whole surface is thoroughly damp. To ensure an even coverage, spray from side to side, backwards and forwards, up and down.

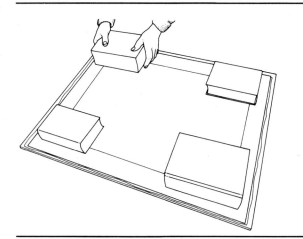

Step 2

Pat away excess moisture and lay the map, front side up, between sheets of fresh blotting paper on a flat, firm board. Place a sheet of glass over the top, then a weight such as a brick or books at each corner. Smaller pictures will need only one weight, but the glass must be pressed flat over the whole area.

Step 3

Coat the ready-made and sanded wooden frame with red acrylic paint. Put the paint on fairly thickly to make sure that all the wood is covered, and brush out the more obvious ridge marks made by the bristles during painting. Acrylic paint will naturally dry to a flat finish. Set the frame aside to dry thoroughly.

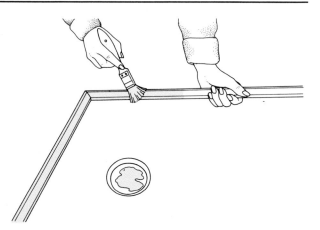

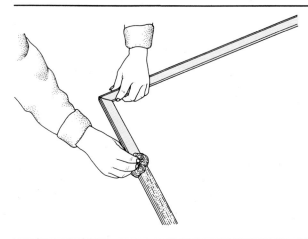

Step 4

A mid-shade of gold wax mixed with turpentine is then applied over the red base and allowed to dry. Next, take a small wad of fine steel wool and rub the surface in one continuous line, lightly at first, until you see how much pressure will remove enough of the gilt to reveal the underpaint in fine streaks. For a variation, rub the steel wool in the opposite direction across the frame in some areas using the same pressure. Continue this action overall, being careful not to rub away too much gold paint in any one area.

Above: The different paint finishes to the frame for the map: one small off-cut of moulding shows the red base coat, and the other shows the gold paint added and rubbed back; the made-up frame is being stippled with the stiff brush dipped in umber, after which the dark green spatter will be applied.

pull paper which is expanded and pulpy with water, as the shrinkage that occurs when it dries may cause ripples or stretch-marks when the intention was to remove them.

If the inside section of the paper seems taut and the outer edges loose (even though wet), it is better to tape it to the board with small pieces of tape at each corner, then fill in the tape around the remaining sides. Leave the picture until it is completely dry. Whichever of these methods is used, the tape must be removed very cautiously and slowly or it will tear the surface of the paper.

Repairs to paper can be done individually, using a strong conservation tissue or mulberry paper and flour paste, as described in Step 7. It is easier to achieve a perfect result if the tear is fresh, because the edges of an old tear may have worn away and so will not meet to form a neat line. If the tear has browned or dirty edges which should be removed, trim them lightly with a sharp blade before the patch is applied to the back of the paper.

It is important to use a type of adhesive that will not affect the paper adversely and will not de-

Step 5

After dabbing on the third, stippled colour, and allowing it to dry, mix paint of a contrasting colour, neither too liquid nor too stiff, on a shallow dish or piece of glass. Dab a fairly stiff brush into this paint, just enough to collect colour on the tip. Hold a small piece of stiff card in one hand a few centimetres above the frame and flick the tip of the brush against the edge of the card so that the paint spatters downwards. The result varies according to the angle at which the card is held, its distance from the frame, and the liquidity of the paint.

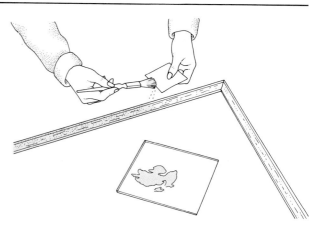

Step 6

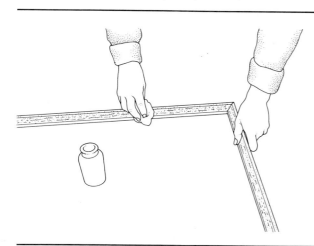

Dip a wad of cotton wool into liquid french polish until saturated and apply it to the top of the frame in one continuous sweep. As this type of polish dries quickly, it is important not to go back over it or the fibres of the wool will catch and stick to the polish. Repeat with each side of the frame, and wipe away excess polish underneath the frame with a rag moistened with white spirit. This polish provides a tough protective finish.

Step 7

To mend a small tear, lay the piece of art face down on waxed tissue paper on a flat surface. Cut a piece of mulberry or conservation tissue paper large enough to bridge the tear on all sides and fray the edges slightly with your fingers. Apply flour paste sparingly with a soft clean brush to the frayed paper, holding one edge down with the tip of your finger. Carefully place the paper over the tear, pat down firmly and cover with waxed tissue paper. Put a piece of glass and a light weight on top. Leave to dry.

Step 8

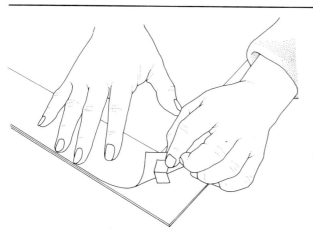

To secure the picture in position in the frame, cut a piece of conservation card the exact size of the image. Place the picture face down on the card, aligning the corners. Moisten a folded stamp hinge, attach one half to a corner of the map then carefully press down the other half onto the card. Repeat with the other three corners.

teriorate with time. For this reason, ordinary adhesive tapes are not at all suitable. A simple paste, free of impurities, can be made very easily by mixing one part of wheat flour with ten parts water. The flour is blended first with a little cold water to a smooth paste, placed in a double saucepan (or a container within a pan of water) so that it is not over direct heat. Boil the remaining water and add to the mixture. Stir rapidly until the paste begins to thicken, then put it back on the heat to thicken more. A very small amount of 40 per cent formaldehyde solution, obtainable from most chemists (pharmacists), added to this paste will make it mould- or mildew resistant.

Waxed tissue paper interleaved between the repair section and the flat surfaces on each side will prevent any paste which might seep through from sticking to them. It can be peeled away once the repair is dry. This type of paper is available at shops selling packaging and card materials.

A slightly different problem arises when there is a hole to be repaired or the edges of a tear will not meet. There are two ways of dealing with this, demanding a little more time and patience, but the results are very satisfactory when an 'invisible' mend is required.

In the first case, paper as near as possible to the original in texture and colour is shredded down to a fine powder and mixed with flour paste. It is then applied to the hole or gap (over the already patched area) and flattened into place with a palette knife or spatula. After this has been weighted and dried, the area can be retouched as necessary.

An alternative is to use fine cotton wool, broken up into small pieces and laid onto the missing area after the paste has been applied lightly with a fine-tipped brush. This method is appropriate where the tear meets only in part, leaving gaps at intervals. The fibres of cotton wool which have not been caught into the glue can be trimmed away with a sharp blade after the repair has dried.

Badly-damaged paper which is not valuable and which has many tears may be sealed by ironing thermo-plastic tissue onto the surface, at the same time preventing future damage. Thermo-plastic, which softens under heat and hardens to a tough finish when cooled, is obtainable from craft and hardware stores or those specializing in plastics.

Less valuable work can also be glued down onto a backing of conservation card. Paste is put on the card first and the picture placed over it. The torn edges are carefully eased together with, if necessary, a little paste dabbed onto the edges which can then be pressed into position for a neat finish.

Although a picture without the support of an actual mount will be kept fairly flat by being sandwiched between the glass and the backing board, it should be hinged onto an intermediate support, following the instructions in Step 8. Stamp hinges are ideal for this as they do the job with a minimum of adhesion. Conservation card is the best backing to use because it is acid-free. A piece of hardboard (masonite) will provide the final backing.

When planning a suitable frame consider, as usual, the object's age and subject matter. Although your repaired and flattened picture may not necessarily be of a great age, the old, slightly discoloured map shown here needs a surround in keeping with its period.

The size of the picture must also be taken into account. An unusual combination of colours applied to a thin frame will obviously look restrained, whereas the same effect applied to a wider moulding may be too overpowering, especially if the overall frame and picture are small. A very large picture need not necessarily have a wide thick frame, however, but to gain a satisfactory effect of an interesting colour mixture on the frame it should be wide enough to make them easily visible.

A fairly broad and heavy moulding with a dark stain could look most effective on a very old decorative map or a facsimile, as that would probably have been the original type of framing used. In contrast, a map printed in black and white only is often framed in a simple thin black bead or flat moulding. A thin gilt or silver, or stained wood might also be practical and appropriate. Nevertheless, there are more enterprising and unusual finishes which are not difficult to apply, and which can be subtle enough not to overpower, for instance, the fine line work or delicate water-colour of our map.

The colour combination chosen for the frame described here consists of four colours applied one on top of the other in different ways: first the base coat; then the second colour, rubbed back; the third colour stippled on and the fourth spattered on. The whole frame is afterwards sealed with a polish or lacquer which also provides a shiny finish.

With the use of four colours there is an endless variety of possible combinations. As it might be rather difficult to foresee the result of so many colours added together, it is important to try them out on a spare piece of moulding to avoid possible disappointment. Varying amounts of the base coat and the second colour can be shown, depending, of course, on how much of the second colour is rubbed away. These two colours should ideally be fairly close in tone and not too contrasting in colour, otherwise the effect could be over-decorative. If the two final colours – stippled and spattered – are applied sparingly, they can afford to be brighter or more contrasting. They will be less evident but will still help to achieve an interesting result.

It is easier to control the application of various colours on a simple, flat or curved moulding rather than a more ornate one. The moulding used here is almost flat but with a small ridge at its outer edge, and it is about 2.5 cm (1 in) wide.

There are a number of alternatives for the first colour, although it should obviously be one which is repeated in the picture. Colours such as blue, red, orange, black or green would be the most useful for a base coat. The second colour could be chosen from the range of liquid metallic paints – gold through bronze to silver – but it must not be applied too heavily as part of it is to be rubbed away.

As usual, the colours chosen for this frame echo and enrich those in the map itself. The base colour is

Left: The old map has been flattened, repaired and set in the painted, antiqued frame hanging above a polished sideboard with intricate inlaid wood. The subtle combination of red, green, brown and gold on the frame is repeated in the fine details of the map.

red to repeat the small red lines in the picture, but it is dulled slightly by adding a little green, making it a brownish-red. The second colour is a mid-tone of gold wax (neither too yellow nor too pink) which blends well with the red. To prevent the whole effect from being too warm, however, the third colour is a darkish umber and the final colour is a dark green.

The first two colours are applied by painting on a heavy first coat and then rubbing back a lighter second coat with steel (wire) wool. The stippled effect of the third colour is achieved by dabbing on the paint with a coarse brush held perpendicularly to the moulding. The fourth colour is then spattered on as described in Step 5. The paint mixtures for both the last two stages should be fairly viscous and applied unevenly, as the charm of this type of finish lies in its 'antiqued' and slightly rough appearance.

Fitting the picture into the frame is done in the same way as for Project 2, with backing board and glass. If the picture is large and heavy, however, it might be a good idea to consider using a different type of hanging attachment from the ordinary screw eyes. Back hangers can be attached to the back of the frame provided it is wide enough. 'D' rings should be attached to the backing board if the frame is narrow; the rivets are inserted through holes made in the board, then hammered under.

Project 6
Silvered Frame for
an Engraving

A large number of older works on paper are often discoloured due to atmospheric conditions, inadequate protective framing or simply the deterioration of the paper. Dampness and humidity causes fungus and mildew growth in paper. In advanced stages, there will be greyish blotches with a pronounced texture of mould. The brown spots known as foxing are caused by a chemical reaction on the iron content of the paper. The spots will increase with time unless the process is arrested. Many water-colours, drawings, engravings, etchings or pastels suffer from such unsightly and damaging markings. It is possible to clean and refresh these pictures, before mounting and framing them in the normal way.

Always examine such pictures carefully before beginning cleaning operations. If the work is extremely discoloured, the cleaning may not give a perfect result but it will certainly improve the appearance a great deal. It is relatively safe and easy to clean prints such as etchings and engravings with a solution of bleach, because printing ink is normally insoluble and will not run. However, hand-coloured work, water-colours, pastels or charcoal drawings must be approached in a different way. Ink drawings may easily run, as will ink signatures on prints, whereas pencil will remain unaffected. A thicker, stronger type of paper will obviously be easier to deal with than a thinner one.

A typical example of an old, discoloured work is this large black and white Victorian engraving of a domestic scene with a finely-written title beneath the picture. The margins outside the picture area and plate-marks are 8–10 cm (3–4 in) wide. It has small brown spots and brown streaks on the reverse side which show through to the front. This engraving was cleaned by bleaching, flattened and mounted with a cut-out opening to show the title, then framed with an antiqued finish suitable to a picture of this particular era.

All marked paper-based work should first be surface cleaned to remove finger marks or smudges (see Project 5) by softly rubbing with a kneadable eraser. Take care not to remove parts of the drawing itself if it is pencil, charcoal or pastel, and avoid delicate or faded signatures such as those on old etchings or more recent lithographs and screen-prints. If this surface dirt is not removed it may become more ingrained after cleaning with liquid bleach.

The sterilizing properties of bleach are invaluable as a preventive to further contamination. There are many types of bleaching agent, some stronger and

quicker-acting than others where a thorough rinsing is necessary after treatment. I would recommend Chloramine T because of its mildness, its slowness of action, and the fact that rinsing is not necessary if the solution is weak. A 5 ml (1 teaspoon) measure of the powder dissolved in 1 litre (2 pints, 5 cups) of distilled water is a good proportion. After some experience, the mixture may be strengthened if necessary.

Before beginning any cleaning, test a small part of the paper, perhaps at the edge, to make sure there are no unforeseen dangers. Some delicate paper will disintegrate when dampened. Professional restorers put fine papers in an airtight box or cabinet with a lamp and thymol crystals (a fungicide from distilled oil of thyme) in a saucer. The warmth melts the crystals and the vapours clean and sterilize the picture. This is used particularly for pictures of great value on tissue-thin paper.

Bleach solution can be applied by soft brush, atomizer spray, cotton wool (cotton) swabs or bathing in a shallow try (Step 1). Water-colours, ink, charcoal or pastel drawings and others where the colour or surface texture is endangered by immersion in water should be bleached by using an atomizer spray, evenly from side to side of the picture which is first laid on blotting paper, as fully described in Project 5. The spray should not be aimed directly at the picture as the current of air caused by the blowing action may dislodge loose particles from a pastel or chalk drawing. Allow the work to dry out before a second application.

Applying bleach with cotton wool swabs is less satisfactory as it is difficult to apply evenly. Also, if the picture is badly stained the brownness will be lifted and transferred by the cotton wool which must be changed frequently as it picks up dirt. Individual spots which remain obstinate when the rest of the work has cleaned up well can be stippled with the solution, using a fine-tipped soft hair brush. Stipple these spots while the rest of the paper is damp, during each application, but do not saturate them or rings will form as the stains spread outwards.

When there is doubt about the picture's vulnerability, apart from the paper quality, the bleach can be applied to the back of the work, particularly when it is obvious that the damage has originated from the back, or if there is danger of the colour running. The result is often successful unless the paper is glued to a card backing and its removal is a tricky job which should be left to a professional restorer.

Etchings and engravings printed with oil-based ink can be safely laid in a bath of bleach solution without fear of the ink running, as long as the paper is strong enough. Whether the paper is thick or thin, it is wise to slide a piece of glass or a thick plastic sheet underneath to lift it out of the bath. This will support the paper when it is pulpy with water and therefore weakened. The paper should never be lifted out by hand at the corners because of the strain caused by the extra weight of the water. Submerged paper must be watched carefully and left only for a brief time. The picture can be allowed to dry and the operation repeated if necessary.

Left: A charming Victorian engraving, The Minuet, in its original dark brown and black frame with gilt slip. The picture has no mount, and some of the grime is obviously surface dirt trapped beneath the glass, but the engraving also has light foxing and heavier brown streaks probably caused by resin seeping through the back of the paper from the rough wooden backing board. The picture needs to be cleaned by bleaching, then mounted and re-framed with fresh glass, and the rough backing replaced by hardboard.

Step 1

The brown stains and foxing are to be removed from the print by bleaching. Carefully tip the engraving into a large, shallow plastic tray containing enough bleach solution to cover the paper entirely and make sure it is submerged. After twenty minutes or so, depending on the strength of the mixture, remove the engraving by sliding a piece of glass under the paper and lifting it out of the bath, supporting the paper lightly with one finger so that it does not slide off the glass. Transfer the engraving to a flat surface of blotting paper and allow it to dry.

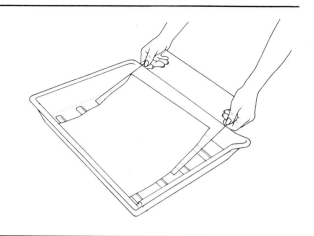

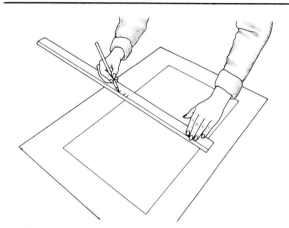

Step 2

The opening for the engraving is drawn up on the back of the mount card. Now mark off the horizontal part of the little opening and start to make the criss-cross lines to form a grid for it on the card. Then mark off the vertical section, keeping the same balance of space around the writing as for the horizontal, but allow for extensions or twirls on individual letters.

Step 3

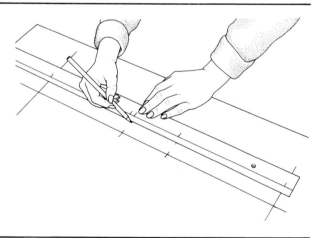

Draw up the grid for the title opening by joining the four corners together with pencil. Make sure that the title opening is central and positioned evenly in relation to the larger engraving opening by checking the distances on each side.

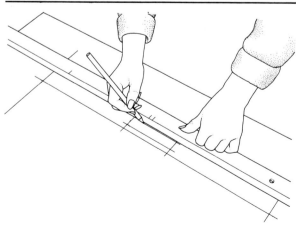

Step 4

Check all the lines of both engraving and title openings with a set square and ruler to make sure they are running straight. Cut out the larger opening with a knife and steel ruler, then cut out the title opening, working in clockwise fashion to avoid cutting the bevel the wrong way round. Precision is essential as any slight ripple in the bevel will be more noticeable on this small scale than on the larger opening.

Step 5

Carefully position the mount over the picture so that there are even amounts of space around both the image and the title openings. This engraving is slightly off square and it is necessary to swing the mount a little and position it so that there is not too much space on any one side. However, it is visually better to have the horizontal edges running straight, especially the one immediately below the print as it is generally more noticeable.

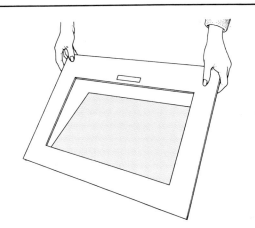

Step 6

To dull a bright silver leaf frame, first rub back a minimal amount with steel wool and then mix a little antiquing paste in a saucer and stipple it on sparingly with a coarse bristle brush held perpendicularly to the length of the frame, using a light, short brushing motion. Continue right around the frame in this manner. A little turpentine in the saucer will help if the mixture is too stiff to apply easily. If the overall effect needs softening or varying, the paste can be rubbed along the frame with cloth wrapped around your finger.

Spots which are bleached from coloured areas will reveal the colour of the paper underneath and will also stand out more definitely as spots than if they had not been cleaned. This calls for retouching which can be a difficult task, especially to a water-colour. Such retouching is often a matter of improvisation, for although it is possible to match the colour and tone, it is much harder to match the surface texture with the original. Even with pastel retouching, the grain of a freshly-applied pastel will be noticeably different if observed from a side angle, and needs to be scraped or rubbed in to help it blend with the original.

Another problem is fly-spots which occur on old paper-work that has been left uncovered or displayed without glass as a protection. Such spots can be removed by a mixture of equal parts of hydrogen peroxide and ordinary ether, available at chemists (pharmacists), shaken together so that the impurities sink to the bottom of the container. The spots are stippled with a fine brush dipped in the top layer of the solution.

After cleaning by any of these methods, the paper should be flattened as described in Project 5, using whichever of those processes that seems most appropriate.

If the picture was so dirty or stained that it has not cleaned up completely, choose a mount (mat) colour that will minimize the fact. Fresh pale colours should be avoided, as they will make a brownish paper seen even darker. Instead, muted and mixed tones of grey, green or beige are more suitable. Another alternative would be a strong contrast in a deeper colour, such as dark green or brown, as dark colours tend to make pale paper seem even paler.

When choosing the mount colour, however, do not sacrifice the needs of the colours within the picture for the needs of its paper. It is obviously easier to choose a mount colour for a black and white print such as this Victorian engraving which cleaned up very well, thus lending itself to an almost unlimited choice of colours. A medium blue-green was eventually chosen. As the print is fairly dark in tone, the fine lines giving a density to the shadowed areas of the composition, this colour gives the whole picture a necessary lift without being too bright.

The width of the mount and its proportions to the picture area must be considered next. The picture area of an old print may have cleaned rather better than its margins, and if the picture is 'busy' any remaining staining will be less obvious. It is normal to have the mount opening just outside the plate-marks - between 3–10 mm ($\frac{1}{8}$–$\frac{3}{8}$ in) or so – or enough to take in any writing surrounding the picture. The mount will therefore conceal odd blemishes on the margin.

The margins of the mount here are 6.5 cm ($2\frac{1}{2}$ in) at top and sides, and 9 cm ($3\frac{1}{2}$ in) at the bottom. The extra width on the bottom is needed to take in the cut-out opening for the title which would look very cramped if it were the same as the other three sides.

To obtain the size of the opening for the picture

measure the engraving vertically and horizontally, plus about 6 mm ($\frac{1}{4}$ in) of its own white surround. The intended margin widths can then be added to give the overall mount size, as described in Project 2. As the engraving may not be truly square, check each side in at least two places. This title opening is an individual cut-out, convenient because the writing is not very close up to the picture. However, writing which *is* close to the picture will not leave enough space for such an opening, so a more suitable cut-out would be merely an extension of the picture opening, the cutting line travelling down, around the writing and up again. Establish the vertical size of the title opening, allowing a little space around the writing so that it will not look cramped, then plot the horizontal size. All the measurements can then be drawn up and the openings cut as in Steps 3 to 4.

Although the frame for an old print need not necessarily be a period facsimile, it will look wrong if it is not compatible with the nature or mood of the composition. A flat, modern gilt or silver finish, for instance, may look well on a modern lithograph or screen-print, but it lacks the little bit of extra finesse and decoration or 'aged' patina which complements older pictures.

The frame chosen for our Victorian picture is a ready-prepared moulding, approximately 3 cm ($1\frac{1}{4}$ in) wide, with fine variations in the contour, and a dull silver leaf finish. Even so, the silver seemed a little too raw and bright for the muted tones of the picture, but scratching a section of the moulding revealed a dark reddish-brown base colour. The silver was therefore rubbed back slightly with steel wool to reveal some of the brown, so breaking up the solid silver surface. Then a commercial antiquing paste, the kind used on furniture, was put on to make the silver even duller. A black paste was chosen to complement the black of the engraving. The combination of dark brown and black gives an interesting result, though not too unusual as to draw the attention away from the engraving. It is probably wise to seal the frame with some kind of finish, perhaps a clear lacquer as used in previous projects.

Project 7
Glass Trap for a
Double Sided Script

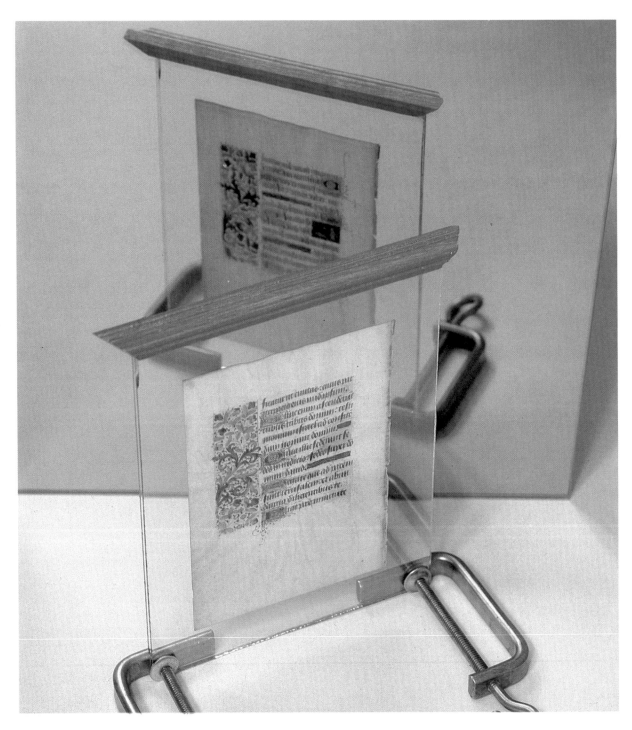

Many pictorial items have something of interest on the reverse as well as the front, and would obviously benefit from being framed so that both sides are visible. This category includes script or music sheets, double-sided drawings or water-colours from a sketch-book, perhaps signed posters from a historic exhibition, menus from a famous restaurant, theatre programmes, poems, letters, anniversary messages or even personal cards – in fact, any pieces with writing on the back which would lose half their appeal if covered with a backing board.

For such two-way display the frame is made in the normal way, but the piece of art is pinned into it between two sheets of glass instead of one, so that it can be turned around and hung on either side. This type of frame is called a glass trap. The picture is held in position by very small pieces of double-sided tape or stamp hinges attached to the glass (so that it can easily be removed later, if need be). The frame can be made to fit the picture exactly, or it can be made slightly larger on all sides, in which case the glass will also be larger all round the art work, giving it a 'floating' appearance. The rebate (rabbet) area of the frame must be deep enough to take the two pieces of glass with enough space for the nails to pin the glass in firmly.

An alternative is to mount the picture before placing it between the glass pieces. This involves cutting two mounts (mats) and placing them back to back with the picture in between. The mounts need not necessarily be the same size on the inner edges, although they must obviously be the same outer size to fit the frame. If the picture or script edges differ on each side, it may look better if the inner sizes are cut to fit each side. However, check the thickness of the paper first. If it is very thin the portion of the smaller mount which is not covered by the larger one will be visible from the other side.

Another essential point is to make sure that the thickness of the combined mounts and pieces of glass will fit easily into the frame. The depth of the rebated area of the frame will need to be roughly twice that needed for two pieces of glass. Smaller frames normally carry a shallower rebated area than larger ones, so if you intend to double-mount the picture, choose the moulding carefully.

It is also possible to have a 'double' frame by making two frames of the same size and joining them together, with the picture and pieces of glass sandwiched between them. This could be the answer to the awkward problem of fitting a double mount and double glass into one frame. It does, however, call for precision in measuring the thickness of the component pieces – glass and card – and comparing this with the measurement of the two rebate depths added together, because the components must fit into the frames exactly with no free space. Otherwise they will be loose and slide around, letting dust specks enter more easily which could spoil the whole effect.

A 'double' frame of this kind can be joined together by inserting nails through one frame and into the other, with the nail-heads sunk below the surface as for corner-joining. The holes can then be plugged and retouched, so that the joining is invisible. It may be convenient, however, to use screws instead of nails in case the whole framing needs to be taken apart at a later date. Obviously, the holes will have to be placed carefully to avoid being too close to the rebated area where the glass fits. To prevent accidents, drill the holes before fitting their glass pieces and picture into the frame.

A free-standing glass trap may be preferred for some double-sided pictures which are viewed more easily on a table or shelves than hanging on a wall. The pieces of glass with picture inside are slotted into a wooden stand consisting of two moulding sections glued back to back so that the two rebated areas are facing each other. As there is no all-round frame here, do not cut the glass yourself which gives it rough edges, but take it to a glazier for a smooth finish. Careful measuring is again necessary to ensure that the slotted area is the exact width to fit the glass and picture snugly so that they do not slip about. The moulding is cut to the same width as the glass and coloured or stained for an attractive finish.

The stand must be solid at the base so that it will not topple over. It is therefore more important to have a deep moulding rather than a wide one, in that the base of the stand is actually the side of the moulding. The type of architectural moulding sold by most wood merchants, without a rebate, would be perfectly suitable for such a stand as it is usually thicker and heavier than picture-frame moulding, consequently providing a more solid foundation. As there is no rebate to hold the two pieces of glass, a piece of wood, cut to the required width and length, should be glued between the two pieces of moulding.

As usual, the composition of the picture is all-important when deciding upon the type of frame, its colour and width. Pieces of script or sheet music which have predominantly black figures on a white or other pale paper, for instance, could look simple but effective in a plain black frame. If this seems a little too severe, a simple moulding with a plain but contrasting colour such as red might be more cheerful.

A painted glass mount gives an unusual and dramatic effect, especially a black surround for a black and white picture. This is created by spraying or painting black lacquer onto the inside of the piece of glass. First determine the position of the picture on the glass and cover this area with masking tape, so that the paint will not go over it. Any slight crookedness of the line on the black inner edge will be very noticeable, so position the tape accurately. After the lacquer has dried, the tape is removed slowly and cautiously to prevent the paint from breaking away.

Left: The glass trap method of displaying a picture is demonstrated here with the aid of a mirror to show the reverse side of this small decorative script on vellum. The picture is clamped between two sheets of glass with one piece of the intended moulding to show the shape of the frame when it is made up.

Step 1

Place one of the cut pieces of glass flat on the table with the picture on top. With the help of a ruler laid across picture and glass, centre the picture so that the surround of glass is equal on all sides. When the position is accurate make small marks with a felt tip pen (or chinagraph pencil) on the glass at each corner of the picture. These marks can be wiped off afterwards.

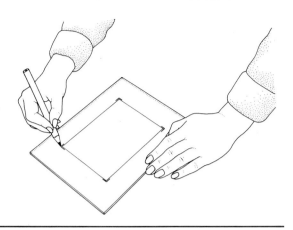

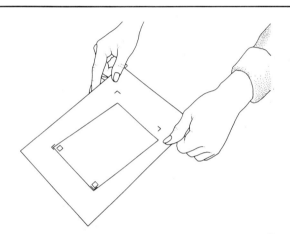

Step 2

Turn the glass over so that the markings are on the reverse side. Attach tiny stamp hinges or pieces of double-sided tape to each upper corner of the picture, but not beyond its edge. Clean the upper side of the glass and place the picture on it, aligning the corners with the markings which you can see through the glass. Press the picture onto the glass so that the hinges stick lightly. The other piece of glass is then laid on top, and the marks on the glass rubbed off.

Step 3

With the frame made and painted, add the profile lines of colour. Using a small lining fitch brush or flat thin brush, run the paint along the channel of the frame (the width of the channel determines the size of brush to use). Apply fairly liberally and evenly, not worrying if the paint spills over the edges a little. Wipe off any excess as soon as possible (see Step 4), as the paint dries quickly and is difficult to remove once dry.

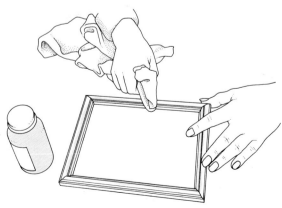

Step 4

Bind your first finger tightly with a small piece of light cloth and draw it firmly along one side of the moulding so that the finger bridges the gap, thus removing the excess paint from the edges. It is important to draw the cloth along without lifting it, otherwise smearing will result instead of a clean, straight line. As the cloth becomes clogged with paint change frequently to a fresh piece. If the paint is drying out too quickly, moisten the rag a little with water.

Step 5

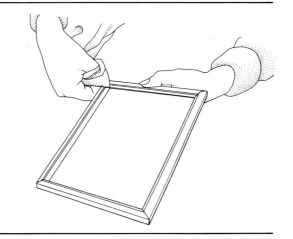

By the time you have worked round the frame and arrived at the first corner again, the paint should be almost dry. To clean away any paint which has built up in the corners, bind your thumb with cloth and draw lightly with the thumb-nail along each ridge, starting from the corner and working away from it.

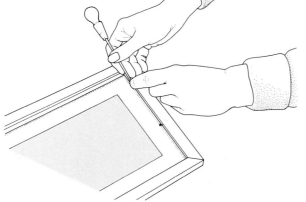

Step 6

Holes have been punched all round the frame. Place the glass sheets and picture back into the frame, and insert a panel pin into a hole, keeping it in position with one finger while steadying the frame with your thumb on the outside. Using a flat metal object such as square-headed pliers, not a hammer which might shatter the glass, press the pin in straight and flat against the glass until it does not extend beyond the inner edge of the frame which can be seen through the glass on the reverse side.

Step 7

Moisten a strip of the gold-painted brown paper with a damp sponge and place one edge down first so that it covers the pins completely. It must also align with the inner edge of the frame which can be seen through the glass on the other side. Now press the rest of the paper down and over the back of the frame to its outer edge to make a neat finish. Repeat all round. The corners may need to be cut slightly and eased together while still damp.

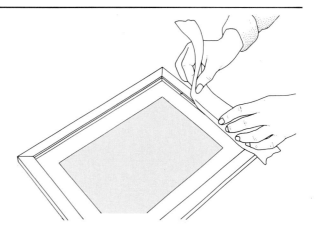

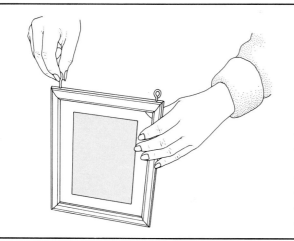

Step 8

Using the width of the moulding as a guide, mark this measurement at the same distance in from each side on the top of the frame in the thicker, central part of the wood with a pencil. Punch holes for the rings with a bradawl. To achieve an overall effect, the steel screw eyes can be painted the same colour as the backing paper. Now screw the rings into the frame so that the thread of the screw is embedded in the wood.

Project 7

Interesting variations can be made by masking off smaller bands, using thinner tape, then painting the resultant strips in a contrasting colour such as gold lacquer. This combination has the same effect as the 'line and wash' technique (see Project 2). It is a painstaking task and difficult to do well without a certain amount of practice.

The object shown in our glass trap is a small double-sided page of old script on vellum, with fine, delicate writing containing decorative flourishes. As the vellum is rather buckled and brittle with age and could easily crack, it would be unwise to try flattening it out. Vellum should not be subjected to moisture; it tends to shrink when exposed to water and the nature of the skin means that varying thicknesses contract in different ways.

Because this picture is so small, it needs a 'floating' frame, created by leaving a margin of glass about 4 cm (1½ in) on all sides of the vellum. A mount (or mounts) would be too strong for such delicate work, and there is a fair amount of space around the writing in any case, which provides a 'self mount'.

The shape and size of moulding for this script needs to be simple and narrow. The chosen frame is about 20 mm (¾ in) wide, a shallow reverse or falling-away type with small ridges on it. Although the frame could be attractive if painted in one delicate colour only, this particular shape was chosen so that lines of a contrasting colour could be added to the dips or channels between the ridges and the other parts of the frame. Indeed, one solid colour would be too heavy on a picture with such soft and fine line work, and the surface of the frame needs to be broken up a little.

A liquid gold paint was used here to echo the gilt in the script, with two thin blue lines added to enrich the effect. These pick up the blue in flourishes of the writing. There is not enough green in the script to warrant green lines, and the red is too close to the gold of the frame to provide a satisfying contrast. As the frame will be protected by lacquer, the blue was a little lighter in tone than the writing to allow for a slight darkening caused by the lacquer.

The frame is made up and painted in the usual way. Always remember to sand and smooth the moulding. If liquid gold is used, it may be necessary to stir it continually to prevent the gold grains separating from the liquid. Lacquer-based paint will dry very quickly and should be applied with a full brush to avoid having to go over the same piece twice.

Once the frame has dried, hold it against the picture to decide whether the addition of one or two lines, sometimes called 'profile' lines, would be an improvement. Some of the many possible combinations include a silver or gold base with black, olive green, red, dark brown or off-white lines. Some moulding shapes, such as a small one with an inner dip curving from the outer edge down to the inner, lend themselves well to quite a broad band of colour. In such a case the centre part can be painted, leaving the base colour on either side.

Acrylic paint, which can be diluted with water if the consistency is too stiff, is the most convenient for painting 'profile' lines. By using the method described in Steps 3–5, the band of colour will be clear and straight along the edges as well as being easier to apply. This will avoid the painful business of attempting to paint the line straight by free-hand. With a small frame like this, apply the colour to one length of the moulding at a time wiping away the excess paint before it dries. Acrylic paint hardens quickly, so it is important not to leave the edges unfinished. If the frame is large, however, the painting and cleaning-off should be done in sections of, say, 15 cm (6 in) or so.

The two inner sides of the glass must be particularly well cleaned if the 'floating' glass trap method is used, because any smudges or finger-marks will be very obvious on the 'see-through' part of the glass when the two pieces are fitted together. Sometimes, as here, any wrinkles on the vellum are smoothed out a little when the pieces of glass are pressed together. This also helps to spread the effect of the wrinkles over the whole picture making them less obvious than if they were concentrated in one particular area.

Before nailing the glass and picture components into the frame (Step 6), first plot for the panel pins. By placing the glass in the frame and marking the position for one hole, you can determine the exact level for the nail to hold the glass firmly in place. It is then safer to remove the glass and punch holes all the way round on the same level as the first one. Small 1 cm (⅜ in) brads are normally long enough for this job. They must not show after the picture is assembled, and they must be driven in flat and straight for a neat finish. A good way to get the exact depth of the hole is to measure a brad against the tip of the bradawl and mark off half its length on the bradawl with a brightly-coloured felt tip (fibre) pen, then punch holes until this point is reached.

An alternative way to secure the glass is to cut small fillets of thin wood and glue them into the rebate of the frame on all four sides so that they are against the glass, holding it in place. Each piece should be the length of the rebate hollow, and they should be thin enough not to show from the front of the frame. They can be painted the same colour as the frame so that they blend for a neat effect. It is easier and less messy to paint these slivers before they are fitted.

If the frame is larger, however, the glass will be a good deal heavier, particularly as there are two pieces. In this case, it would be wiser to nail the fillets into place to secure the glass safely. Use the same method for punching the holes and try not to resort to a hammer.

When fillets are used it is unnecessary to paper over the back rebate as they provide quite a neat finish in themselves. However, the nailing-in method shown in the drawings benefits from a thin strip of paper hiding the pins. For this small gilt frame, the strips of brown gummed paper were painted with the same liquid gilt before being applied. It is better not to cut the strips to the exact width as it is difficult to align them correctly on both inner and outer sides at the same time. The over-

Above: The front of the completed glass trap, showing the gold-painted frame with two fine blue lines which repeat the blue ornamental design in the script. The two screw eyes are painted the same colour as the frame. Although the buckle in the vellum has not been removed entirely, the pressure of the two pieces of glass has reduced it to a fine ripple.

Right: The reverse side of the finished glass trap, showing the paper, coloured with gold paint to match the frame, neatly applied to cover the small nails. It is important to paint the paper before it is glued into place, as the paint may otherwise spill over onto the glass and spoil the clean edges.

lapping portion on the outer edges can be trimmed away afterwards.

Ideally the hanging rings should be attached to the top of the frame, thus enabling the picture to be hung either way round. It may be more convenient to use the type of screw eye which has a second loop so that it is more flexible. If you want the method of hanging to be less apparent, insert one ring instead of two, but this is inadequate for the weight of anything but a small, light picture. Also, a single ring must be perfectly centred or the picture will not hang straight. When rings are attached to the top of the frame wire is not necessary as the loops can be hung directly onto the hook on the wall

Project 8
Shadow Box
for a Ceramic

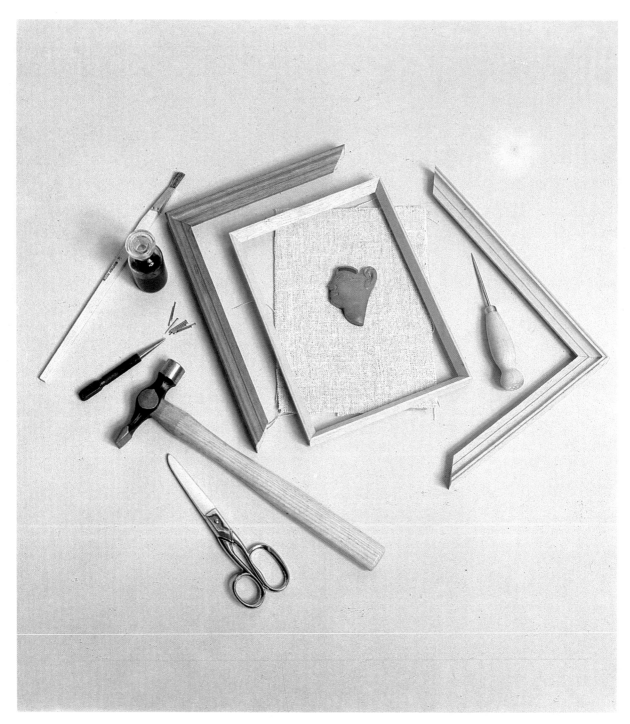

Framing need not be confined to flat art work on paper, board or canvas. Many three-dimensional objects which would look good hanging on a wall cannot be displayed without some kind of support or surround, and a number of these may also need the protection of glass. Included in this range are such items as decorative fans, raised creative embroidery, small sculptures of wood, ivory or stone, ceramics, cluster groups of shells, dried leaves, paper or fabric collage or small relief sculptures that need protection.

Such small treasures are often stored away or left lying in a drawer because they seem insignificant when presented simply as ornaments either on a shelf or grouped with others. They can, however, look most effective in the type of frame known as a shadow box. Here the object is attached to a fabric-covered background and framed in the normal way, but the glass is raised away from it. This is achieved by placing the glass between the outer frame and an inner frame or fillet, so that the glass does not touch the highest point of the object.

Different kinds of shadow box obviously suit different objects. A popular craft work such as a design of shells, stones, seaweed and grasses can be given a more permanent arrangement when glued onto a rigid support. Cover the board first with fabric, perhaps a coarse silk, linen or hessian (burlap) in either a dark colour for a dramatic effect or a soft colour from the range of beige or salmon pinks. A simulated 'beach' background can easily be created by spreading glue on the board and sprinkling it thickly with sand. The same plan could be used for an arrangement of plants, dried flowers or feathers, or a design made of the bark of trees.

Fillets may be more suitable than an inner frame to hold the glass. They can be covered in the same material as the background. A simple moulding with a soft wood stain would be suitable for the outer frame.

Collages, made of paper or fabrics, beads, jewels and other materials, also lend themselves to framing in a shadow box. As the design probably covers the whole board, an inner frame may be more appropriate here than fillets.

A thick embroidery which has raised areas of heavy stitching will be awkward to frame in the conventional manner, and a shallow box effect is preferable to a squashed object. One way of displaying a small embroidery such as a raised sampler, is to sew it to a larger fabric-covered board, thus leaving a decorative margin of the fabric on all sides. It is also useful if the sampler is slightly crooked and will not fit into a square frame easily.

Left: This eighteenth-century ceramic head is attached to a background of linen fabric on board, and surrounded by some of the components and tools necessary to construct a shadow box. The inner frame is joined but not yet painted. One half of the outer frame is also unpainted while the other half has only one coat of wood stain which is not dark enough, so that a further coat will be necessary.

To frame an ornamental fan which is often old and fragile, spread it out and place on a fabric backing, then attach it by invisible stitches at various points so that when it is hanging up it will not flop forward. Most period fans are fairly delicate in design, so appropriate backing fabrics would be velvet or silk, perhaps in a medium tone such as a blue-grey or a colour repeated from the fan. The traditional fan-box is made in the fan shape, or with a curved top and flat lower edge, like a compass. The frame sections are constructed out of thick plywood so that the curved part can be bent into shape. A light beading is added to the top, sometimes incorporating a filigree pattern, and the whole is then gilded. The glass is held in place with fillets, as an inner frame would be unsuitable.

All these objects need glass to protect them from dust which would otherwise collect in small creases or corners. It is also a good idea, in many cases, to fit an overall backing as described in Project 4 so that it can be removed occasionally if the inside needs to be cleaned and dusted.

An alternative way of framing small shallow objects is to buy a ready-made oval or round frame from a choice of dark polished wood, gilt, silver, or black such as those on page 48, with a piece of convex glass which will give an unusual appearance. Choose a size of frame slightly larger than the work; and make sure that the curve of the glass clears the object when the frame is assembled.

Stones, fossils and tiles can be treated similarly, but they may need greater contrast of colouring to set them off. Also, such objects may have a greater depth than the fabric-based items, so deep enough frames must be chosen.

The small ceramic head silhouette framed here was chosen as it is unusual and not an easy piece to frame, particularly as it is rather dull in colour, and simple in shape. A background of coarse linen in a natural light colour fits in with the simple design and is bland enough not to overpower the ochre shade of the head. To enhance the 'earth' feeling the whole framing is kept within a range of brownish tones.

The inner frame is a plain sloping moulding about 13 mm ($\frac{1}{2}$ in) wide, stained with light oak, after which an ochre and umber mixture is added as a thin wash. The outer frame also has an oak stain, with an additional ochre wash. It is about 2.5 cm (1 in) wide, and fairly flat, with two small ridges. To test the effect of this combination, the components were set together with the head in the middle before being actually assembled. As the overall colouring seemed a little too dull, the small inner ridge on the moulding was used to add a thin line of contrasting colour for relief. Introducing an alien colour might be inappropriate, but the dark blue line on this ridge echoing the same colour of the 'eyebrow' on the head is ideal.

As the glass sits between the inner and outer frames, the height of the object (at its uppermost point if the levels vary) must be measured carefully, with a little added to ensure that the glass will not touch it. The depth of the inner frame can then be determined. If the object is not more than 2.5 cm

Step 1

With the linen glued to the backing board, turn the board face down on a clean, flat surface. Trim away the excess V-shape of linen in the corners by cutting straight across just outside each corner at a 45° angle to the sides, but not too close to risk fraying. This will ensure there is no bulky fold of fabric to be glued down. Apply PVA glue with a brush around all sides of the board, enough to take the overlap of linen. Fold back the linen and press it down over the glue so that a neat mitre is formed at each corner.

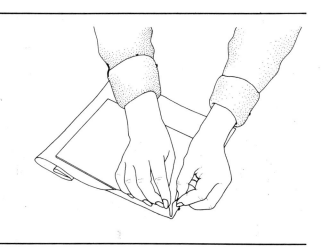

Step 2

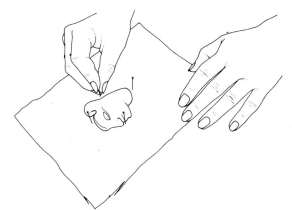

Turn the board face up and, using a ruler to help judge the distance inwards from each side of the board, place the object in a central position. When the exact position is decided, fix small pins at either of the sides or distinct points of the object to serve as a guide. Then attach the object to the fabric with a spot of epoxy resin adhesive. Put a light weight on the object until it dries.

Step 3

With the inner frame made, measure for the outer frame to fit over it. First determine how much of the inner frame is to show. Place a ruler across the frame and mark off the exact measurement, then repeat for the other side. These measurements are 'sight', so you will have to add the exact rebate measurements of the outer frame on all sides so that the outer frame is large enough to take in the inner frame.

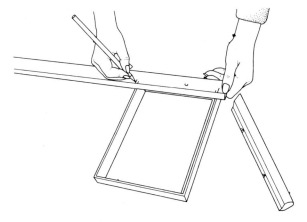

Step 4

To give an extra lift to an otherwise all-over brown frame and to highlight the blue line on the object, a coloured line is added to a small beaded ridge of the outer frame. Hold the frame in place with one hand and draw a chisel-tipped fibre pen along the top of the ridge. Repeat for all sides.

Step 5

Place the glass into the outer frame, followed by the inner frame which is already pinned to the linen-covered board onto which the object is glued or sewn. The frames must be joined together accurately and firmly, and the nails must avoid going too close to the glass or the thin rebate edges of either of the frames. Hold the partly-assembled pieces up and plot the angle of insertion by holding a nail in front of one corner so that you can decide on the length of the nail, where the hole should be drilled and at what angle.

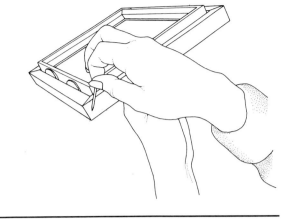

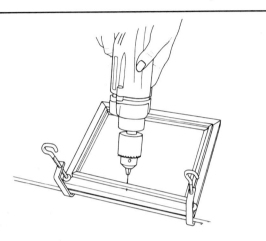

Step 6

With the component pieces – frames, glass and mounted object – held in two clamps, one at each corner, drill a hole at the appropriate angle and to the right depth. To make it easier to know how far to drill, mark the bit with a bright colour. One nail in the centre of each side is adequate for a smaller frame.

Step 7

An overall paper backing makes a neat finish to such a frame. Cut a piece of brown paper slightly larger than the frame at its outer edge. Run a line of PVA glue around the edges of the outer frame, fit one edge of the paper onto it and press down. As the inner frame will be raised above the outer, to obtain a neat finish at the corners, you will need to cut the paper in a mitre shape. Squeeze the edges, one slightly overlapping the other, perhaps with a little extra glue added, then press firmly in place.

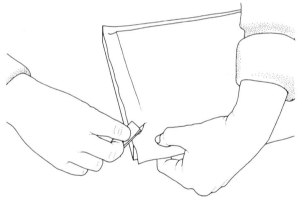

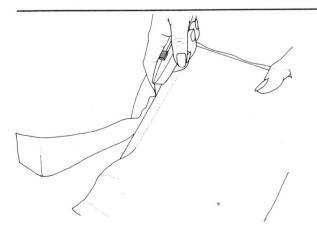

Step 8

After all four sides of the paper have been glued down, the overlapping edges are trimmed away with a sharp knife. Using your first finger pressed against the outer side of the frame as a support, draw the blade along the length of the edge and slightly inwards from it.

(1 in) high, it will be easy to find a type of moulding which is deep enough to cover it, but if the work is much higher it may be necessary to substitute fillets for the inner frame.

Although a deep outer moulding is obviously more convenient for a shadow box, a shallower type may be chosen for its attractive shape or colour, especially if it is a ready-prepared moulding. In this case, it will have to be 'backed up' so that it is deep enough to take the object. Strips of wood are cut to the same size as the frame, the corners mitred and then joined to form a rectangle. This wooden support is then attached to the back of the made-up frame with PVA glue and weights. As glue alone will not be strong enough for a secure joint, nails should also be used. Four holes, one to each side, are drilled from the back, so that they penetrate through the backing wood and a little way into the main frame. Either screws or nails can then be inserted. If there is a crack running around the sides where the two frames join, it should be covered with wood filler for a neat finish. The backed-up section should then be coloured to match the front of the frame.

A collage picture which extends to the edges of the board can be measured as normally for a frame, but items which need to be set against a background should first be placed on the chosen fabric to determine the width of the margins. The aim is to achieve a well-balanced proportion of the surround to the object. Placing a rectangular frame around an object such as a fan, however, gives large background areas at some points and very little at others. With an object of fairly even proportions like this silhouette head it is not difficult to plan the size of the board.

Once this size has been worked out, the board can be cut and the fabric glued to it, in the same way as the poster is glued onto board (see Project 3), but the type of glue must be compatible with the material. A rubber latex adhesive is generally safe as it will not soak through material, a point for concern if you are using thin or open-weave fabric. Here, however, a PVA is satisfactory because the linen is thick with a close weave.

The fabric must be glued to the board before the art is attached to it or else it will not lie flat. Different types of objects are attached to the background in different ways. Software (embroidery or feathers) or articles which provide holes or other leverage, can be sewn onto the fabric. Use a curved upholsterer's needle as a straight one may be hard to manipulate. For heavier articles, the stitches must go right through the board, otherwise the object may drag the fabric away from the board later. If the board is thick, you may need to punch holes and sew through them, but take care to work from the back with a sharp bradawl and avoid unsightly large holes appearing through the fabric on the front.

Stones or small sculptures should be glued to the board. So long as they are light in weight, these should need no more than a spot or two of adhesive, preferably one of the commercial brands such as an epoxy resin, since an ordinary flour paste will obviously not be strong enough.

Making fillets to hold the glass away from three-dimensional objects presents a different problem from constructing an inner frame. The fillets can be made of very thin hardboard (masonite), thick card or balsa wood. The length of each one must be determined accurately, making an allowance for the fabric which is to be attached to it, so that there won't be too tight a fit at the corners. For a neat finish, the fabric should be glued to the fillets with an overlap on all edges (even the corners). The overlap is then turned to the back and glued in place, thus preventing the fabric from fraying, particularly during assembly of the various components.

Ideally, the fillets should be the same width as the rebate (rabbet) of the frame, so that the line is continuous and has no ugly breaks. The measurements for the frame can then be taken from the edges of the board, as the edges of the fillets will be aligned flush with the board too. When the frame is made and coloured, place it face-down and put the cleaned glass into it. The fillets can then be fitted into place, lightly glued to the rebate of the frame, taking care that the glue does not seep out onto the glass.

Measuring for the frame is described in Step 3. When planning the two frames, the outer frame should have a wider rebate width, otherwise there may be an unwanted ridge showing on the inner one. Choose an inner moulding that will fit exactly to the outer one so that the inner gradations travel down smoothly and without a break, as for the fillet fitting into the frame.

If the two frames do not fit exactly, however, fill out the rebate sections with small pieces of cork, as are used in fitting the canvas in Project 1. For this shadow box slivers of cork had to be inserted during assembly, because the thin top section of the inner frame slid too far into the rebate of the outer frame. This made the outer frame jut over the inner one and spoil the smooth inward gradation of the box-like effect.

The colouring on both the inner and outer frames described here is diluted acrylic paint applied over a wood stain. This technique is known as 'liming'. The basic stain is usually darker than the paint wash, and many variations are possible. A rich walnut with a light greenish-grey will give an interesting blend which could suit pictures with warmer tones. A dark oak combined with a light off-white wash will readily complement cooler tones in a picture.

For a liming finish, the stain is first applied to the wood and allowed to dry. The diluted paint is then applied sparingly but firmly with a wad of moistened cotton wool (cotton), which ensures that it sinks well into the grain of the wood. Rub the cotton wool along the wood in a continuous sweep to avoid an uneven application.

The paint, which dries fairly quickly, can be worked over if necessary in either direction but a thin all-over coat is preferable. If the paint is too thick it will take more effort to remove it at the next stage when rubbing it back with steel (wire) wool. The object is to remove traces of this thin layer, leaving a fine residue of paint in the grain of the wood, and combining the wood stain with the paint. Too much

Above: The finished shadow box, with the small head on a linen background set behind the glass which is held away from the object by being inserted between the inner and outer frames. The inner frame is the same colour as the head and several shades lighter than the outer frame which has an ochre wash rubbed into the wood stain to bring the colours of head and frames together.
A little relief from the overall brown effect of the picture is provided by the blue line on the frame which is a restrained repetition of the blue 'eyebrow' on the head.

hard rubbing may well take away the underlying wood stain as well.

If the moulding has a varied contour, lines of the paler wash will remain in the deeper portions where the wire wool cannot reach. This adds an interesting nuance of tone to an otherwise flat colour, particularly if the grain of the wood is close and does not produce much scope for the liming to be effective. The action of the wire wool will give the surface a smooth sheen, but the wood should also have a light waxing.

To assemble the shadow box the two frames must first be pinned together. How they are joined depends on their shape and size. If the inner frame

projects beyond the outer one at the back, they can be firmly and successfully joined as in Steps 5 and 6. In some cases the outer frame will be the deeper of the two, perhaps a 'hockey' moulding (deep-sided with a rounded top), and the frames can be joined by hammering nails in flat as when pinning in a backing board. It is even possible to insert the nails from the side of the outer frame through into the inner one, but the nail heads will have to be sunk, and the holes filled and touched up.

An overall paper backing is used here instead of the paper strips or an overall backing board, because of the different levels in the backs of the frames. The paper should be thick enough not to curl up when it touches the wet glue. Brown wrapping paper is generally adequate. It may wrinkle a little but it will contract as it dries and flatten out.

Despite not having an overall stiff backing the object will fit securely into the box frame because it is already attached to a firm board. The paper backing will seal the entire frame against dust, and provide a neat finish by covering any nails or untidy edges which might be visible from the side when the picture is hanging on the wall. Hanging fixtures should be attached in the usual way to the thicker of the two frames where there is less chance of the wood splitting.

Project 9
Assembling Miniatures in a Gilded Frame

There are many very small decorative items which benefit from being displayed collectively in one frame. These may be round, oval or square miniature paintings such as flowers or portraits on cards, ivory or wood, tiny ceramics, medals, badges or coins. It is preferable if works form a series or are individual pieces of the same type, as the idea of framing two or more objects as a unified whole within one frame depends on their similarity. If they are diverse in colour, design or nature, they will not make a sympathetic and satisfying unity.

Instead of being attached to a flat background as in Project 8, these smaller items can be 'sunk' or embedded into small recessed sections of a fabric backing, so that the surface of each object is level with the surface of the background.

Two oval water-colour miniatures of flowers painted on card were chosen to be framed in this way. As they each had individual gilt miniature frames with convex glass, it was thought best to leave them in these as they provided a neat finish for the two pictures against a fabric background. A hand-gilded outer frame which repeated the gold of the miniature rims seemed a fitting surround.

Ivory miniatures in need of small individual frames may present a problem if they are even slightly too large for bought miniature frames. Whereas paper or card can be trimmed easily if the picture is too big for the frame, ivory is likely to crack if cut. It can be trimmed, however, using a pair of *very* sharp scissors. Pare the ivory in small sections as one would fingernails. The secret of preventing ivory from splitting is to hold it firmly between thumb and forefinger very close to the edge to be cut, and trim tiny sections at a time. It is not a task to be undertaken carelessly.

Making a covered background with recessed areas for the miniatures is simplified by using two pieces of backing. The holes are cut out from the top piece, the under piece acting as a support for the objects when the two boards are stuck together. Thick card from which sections may be cut quite easily is unfortunately not always appropriate. Although coins or objects which are thinner and flatter will need only a shallow bed, miniature paintings need to lie in fairly deep recessions of about 13 mm ($\frac{1}{2}$ in) or so. Polystyrene foam (styrofoam), available in a variety of thicknesses, is therefore ideal. Particularly useful for small frames are the polystyrene 'tiles' normally used to cover cracked walls or ceilings, which are a convenient 10 mm ($\frac{3}{8}$ in) deep.

The foam is very easy to cut because it is soft. Handle with care as it marks easily, and any dents will show through thin covering fabrics such as silk. Most objects look best when they are flush with the background, so if the polystyrene is not the exact

Left: Two miniature water-colours in their own small metal rims are displayed against a piece of brown velvet which is to be their background, surrounded by the half-made, ungilded frame. The velvet will be glued to the polystyrene foam and backed by the solid hardboard.

thickness required for the job, it is better to buy a piece slightly thicker than needed, not thinner. If necessary, padding can be inserted in the recessed areas after the two tiles have been joined together to bring the surface of the objects level with their background. A thick piece of card would serve this purpose, glued neatly into each 'bed'.

Interesting variations can be worked out from the basic method of gluing two tiles together as shown in the line drawings. An alternative method is required, for instance, with miniature paintings which need glass but do not have their own matching small frames. In this case, the pictures and glass are sandwiched between the two tiles, and the holes are cut slightly smaller than the size of the pictures so that glass and pictures will not slip through the openings. First fit the glass to the *back* of the top tile with tiny pieces of masking tape: use the same method used for attaching a picture to a mount (mat), and also attach the picture behind the glass with tape. The second tile is then positioned to form the base.

The edges of the recesses can be varied pleasantly in two ways. If two very thin pieces of foam are used in place of one for the upper section, the holes in the top piece can be cut 6 mm ($\frac{1}{4}$ in) or so larger than the other. When the fabric is stretched over these and glued down, the finished effect will be of a sloping bevelled edge which lends an air of distinction to the framing. However, the fabric must be thick enough for the edge of the outer recess (the larger hole) not to be apparent through it as a hard line. Velvet or a thick linen would be appropriate in this case.

The second alternative method of edging is to make a raised section to encircle the recessed area. A thick twisted cord (such as blind cord or bath-robe cord) is cut to the right length and glued onto the polystyrene around the hole, between 6 mm ($\frac{1}{4}$ in) and 13 mm ($\frac{1}{2}$ in) from the edge, depending on the proportion and size of the recess. The fabric is then glued carefully over the foam and the cord, forming an attractive ridged surround.

Take care too when choosing the type and colour of fabric. The same problems apply as in Project 8 — the material should be closely woven, not too thin or uneven, and capable of accepting an adhesive satisfactorily. You will probably have to consider the choice of colour at the same time, particularly if the material is of a type where there is not a large range to choose from. Small remnants of furnishing fabrics are useful as they are thicker and provide a great range of colour and texture. Buy a piece of material somewhat larger than the estimated overall size of the frame because the exact placement of the objects has not yet been decided, and it would be a pity to crowd them together on a too small piece of fabric.

The two small water-colours here are finely executed and delicately coloured. For such subject matter a smooth plain textured material like silk or velvet is more appropriate than a coarse or knobbly one such as linen or hessian (burlap). These flower studies contain colours which could be repeated in the fabric, but several of them were considered

Step 1

Place the made-up frame over the loose velvet and polystyrene and fit them together temporarily. Position the miniatures not too close together but allowing a larger distance between them and the frame than between each other, use a ruler placed from corner to corner to check that the spaces on all sides are symmetrical, as a slightly lopsided arrangement will be irritating when all the components are fitted together. Make a note of the measurements.

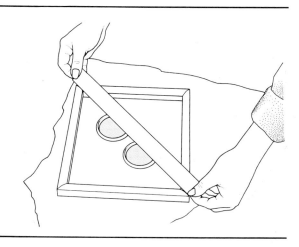

Step 2

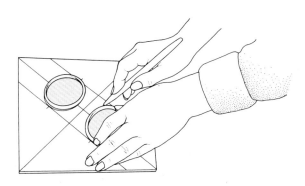

On the uppermost piece of polystyrene, draw lines with a fibre pen from corner to corner diagonally to determine the exact central point. Measure the length of the miniatures, halve this measurement and draw parallel lines on each side of the central horizontal line. Decide the distance needed between the miniatures in the centre, halve this measurement and mark it outwards from each side of the central spot. Put the miniatures in place and draw around them, allowing a hairsbreadth for ease of fitting because the material will overlap the recessed areas and take up some space.

Step 3

Cut around the plotted lines on the polystyrene with a sharp knife and remove the central pieces. The foam is soft and cuts very easily, so a soft, slow action is necessary to avoid jagged edges, and it is harder to control the cutting when the shape is a small oval or round one. The knife must be held straight, not at an angle.

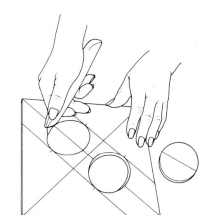

Step 4

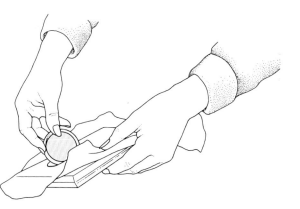

The two pieces of polystyrene are now glued together with epoxy resin adhesive, and the velvet stuck to the upper piece. Cut out the velvet from the centres of the ovals at least 15 mm (⅝ in) inwards from the edge of the polystyrene. Shown here is the three-dimensional effect of the two pieces of polystyrene, the velvet covering and a miniature being slipped into its bed.

Step 5

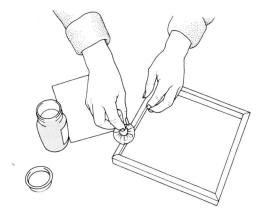

Dip the prepared wad into the size (adhesive) and dab it on a small piece of glass to find the right quantity and consistency which should be tacky. If it is too liquid, allow it to dry out for a minute or two. As the size dries quickly, and applying the leaf is a slow process, work on one side of the frame at a time. Rub the size on firmly to make sure it covers the whole area.

Step 6

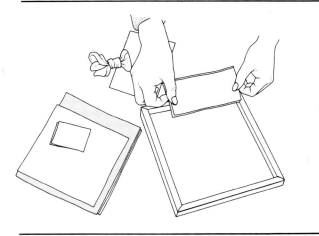

Cut sections of the metal leaf, still on its tissue-paper backing, wide enough to bridge all sides of the moulding in one piece. Carefully and firmly place one piece of leaf onto the frame with the paper side uppermost. Pat it into position and keep firmly in place without removing pressure, as it will take a few seconds to settle and the fragile leaf can tear away easily. Rub a piece of cotton wool over the paper, covering the whole surface and paying especial attention to the edges where the leaf is most likely to tear if it has not gripped properly.

Step 7

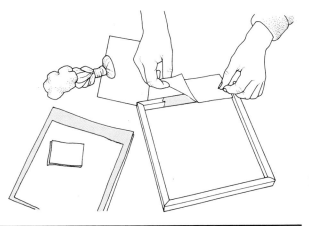

Remove the paper from the gold leaf by lifting one edge first, but watch carefully and have cotton wool ready to tamp down at the slightest sign of the leaf coming away with the paper. If the right amount of size has been applied overall and the leaf is firmly fixed, the paper should lift away easily. Apply the next piece of leaf alongside, but be sure to overlap the first by at least 13 mm (½ in). Now size the other sides of the frame, one by one, and repeat the leaf-laying process.

Step 8

When the whole frame has been gilded, smooth it down firmly with fresh cotton wool. To avoid any stickiness adhering to the cotton wool, have a small amount of fine talcum powder handy. Dab the cotton wool into this lightly and brush off the excess powder against the palm of your hand. Rub the cotton wool gently over the leaf, avoiding areas where it has torn away, as the powder sticking to the size will produce a milky, opaque appearance, and gold leaf should be shiny and clear. Such torn areas can be patched with squares of gold leaf.

inappropriate for such a comparatively large area of background colour, especially the strong shades which could easily overpower delicate work. Of the various colours which could be suitable here, pink might be an obvious choice but it is too bright, and blue or green are also thought to be too strong. The deep chocolate brown shade eventually chosen provides a smooth rich backing, and the thick texture of the velvet enriches this effect still more. Although very dark, this colour offers a dramatic contrast to the subject matter, and serves to highlight the summer tones of the flowers.

Choosing a background colour for medals, coins or small ceramic articles should present less difficulty as they are generally in plain tones, but again they will be better enhanced by a stronger contrast. Miniature portraits look most effective on a background of velvet or silk, but choose a colour that will not sap the skin tones of the subject. In older work of this kind the skin colour is often quite pale, but as the head is usually surrounded by a coloured background, the fabric choice is naturally influenced by this. Perhaps the most suitable colours would be deep brown, rose or muted blue-grey.

If the miniatures are already framed, the shape and colour of the moulding for the overall frame should reflect these small individual surrounds. As our water-colours already had their own tiny gilt frames, a gilt outer frame was chosen to draw the whole composition together. With a dual-framing job such as this it is wise to select a thin plain moulding rather than a more ornate one or else the total effect will be too fussy. Although it is possible to buy a ready-made moulding in rounded or flat shape with either gold or silver metal leaf, mass-produced moulding will not achieve the same personal and individual style as that done by hand. Gold is the obvious choice here, as it not only echoes the small metal rims around the pictures but complements the rich brown fabric.

With the fabric and the objects to hand, decide on the size of the background and where to place the miniatures so that they will fit pleasantly into the overall frame. A certain symmetry in the design is visually satisfying, but it is a mistake to set small objects in a regular pattern with the amount of space between each of them matching the space between them and the frame. And just as it is more interesting to have differences in the space proportions, it is easier to achieve an arresting design if the number of objects is uneven, say, three or five. This was one of the reasons why it was thought best to place the two miniature water-colours so that they would hang diagonally.

When gluing the fabric to the background, the material should be a little bigger than the foam on all sides so that it can be tucked over. If the fabric is very thick, however, the extra bulk may make it difficult to fit into the frame, so it will have to be cut to fit the piece of polystyrene exactly at the edges.

The type of adhesive must be compatible with both the fabric and the foam. An epoxy resin or natural latex adhesive is the most suitable, and either of these are easy to work with. The glue is best applied with a spatula or palette knife and allowed to reach a tacky state before the fabric is laid firmly onto it. When this is quite dry, the centres of the holes can be cut out as described in Step 4.

Different kinds of miniatures are fixed into their 'beds' according to their composition. The same type of adhesive as used for the fabric will stick work such as medals, coins or ceramics. A small dab of the adhesive will usually be enough to hold the object in place, and will make for easier removal later on if the need arises. Fabric-based software miniatures can be sewn into place, after holes have been drilled or punched through the backing so that the thread can be tied firmly on the reverse. The miniatures here have metal flaps which can be pushed through the foam. Other miniature frames usually have their own small backs of thick fabric-covered card, which can be either sewn through or glued into place. Sewing is almost always the preferred method as it is then easier to cut the threads and remove the work without the risk of damage.

Prepare the made-up frame for gilding by smoothing the wood and applying a ready-made acrylic gesso or one made of plaster of Paris mixed with rabbit-skin glue or an equivalent (obtainable from most art stores) to a thick cream consistency, and use while still warm. The ready-mixed variety is convenient and easy to use. For a firm basis that will not crack, apply the gesso in several thin coats rather than one thick one, and allow each coat to dry before the next is put on. Gesso provides a smooth surface for the leaf, but it should be sanded with very fine sandpaper and any dust removed carefully. An acrylic colour such as red, brown or black can be added to it if a base shade for the gold or silver leaf is wanted. When finishing, the golf leaf can be rubbed away to let the colour show through a little.

Two types of leaf are available, metal and real gold. We used the less expensive metal here. The small metal sheets are about 13 cm (5 in) square, and because they are very delicate and light, it is essential to work out of a draught.

The leaf can be applied by either water-glue or oil-size. The gilding process described here is the latter method, using transfer leaf and a special kind of adhesive known as gold size obtainable from craft or do-it-yourself stores. (The type of size used has a 2–4 hour drying-time.) Make a pad for applying the gold size by putting a wad of cotton wool (cotton) inside a piece of rag, and form a handlepiece by twisting the rag round, then seal it firmly with tape. Test that you have the correct amount of size on the wad by dabbing some on a piece of glass, and then rub it firmly onto the frame. It is important not to have too much size on the frame as it will come through the very fragile leaf and mess up the surface. On the other hand if there is not enough size, parts of the leaf will not adhere as it is being tamped down and the result will be an uneven, broken surface.

Much practice is necessary to achieve a perfect result, but charming effects can be achieved by applying the leaf in a deliberately uneven manner, particularly if there is a good base colour. If the piece of leaf is crushed slightly before being applied, for instance, it can form interesting hair-like cracking and crazing effects as the small creases will not adhere but will tear away a little. To ensure that the size does not come through to the surface, the creased areas should not be rubbed too hard. The small folds can be rubbed down and removed *after* the rest of the gilt has dried out completely and hardened to a firm finish.

Another way of laying on gold leaf is by using a soft gilder's 'tip' – a flat brush with short, fine soft hair, usually about 10 cm (4 in) wide and with a card handle. Brush the 'tip' across your skin, the cheek or wrist, which will normally provide just enough grease to allow the leaf to be picked up on the tip of the brush so that it can be transferred to the frame. The merest *hint* of vaseline may be applied to the skin first, if necessary. The leaf can be tamped down very gingerly with a soft, full 'mop-like' hair brush instead of using cotton wool, which should, however, be used to complete the flattening process.

The drying time for the gold leaf may vary according to the temperature, but it is wise to leave it overnight to make sure it is quite set before proceeding to the next step. If the gilt is to be rubbed back to reveal the base colour, this should be done before any protective sealing coat is given. For this frame, the base colour is a dull Indian red mixed with umber, which complements the subject matter and the rich brown velvet backing. As only a few fine lines are needed to break the flat, hard gold surface, very fine steel (wire) wool is rubbed softly and cautiously over the leaf to avoid removing too much of it in any one area.

It is also possible to gild the frame using water-glue, though this method is somewhat lengthier and more complicated. Water-gilding uses a soft red clay known as 'bole' (obtainable from specialist art stores) on the gesso ground to provide a good surface. For a frame the size used here for the minia-tures about 53g (2 oz) of gelatine or rabbit-skin glue is melted in about 1 litre (2 pints, 5 cups) of water into which a lump of bole is mixed. Proportions may vary but one part of bole to four parts of liquid is a satisfactory mixture. Several coats are applied to the gessoed frame, allowing drying time between each one, and the surface is then sanded with fine sand-paper until it is perfectly smooth. Next water is brushed thinly but evenly onto the dry clay with a soft mop brush, partially dissolving the glue and providing a tacky surface for the gold leaf. The surface must not be too damp, however, or the water will soak through the thin leaf. The gold sheets are placed on a padded cushion or 'cush' and cut to size with a sharp knife, then applied to the frame and allowed to dry. The surface can be burnished with an agate (a polished piece of stone) set in a wooden handle to achieve a bright finish.

To protect the delicate leaf and prevent it from becoming tarnished, a clear lacquer is brushed over the frame. A yellow or brownish shade would impart a garish yellow tone and conceal the metallic sheen which is the typical element of gold leaf.

The picture should be fitted to the frame in the

Above: The miniatures set in their velvet surround with a gold-leaf frame rubbed back a little to reveal the red base colour. Hanging the frame as a diamond shape is more unusual than the conventional rectangle or square, and quite attractive so long as the proportions are satisfactory.

most suitable manner. If the frame is not sufficiently deep to take in the thickness of the two pieces of foam and backing board, which will probably be about 2 cm ($\frac{3}{4}$ in) when put together, the method des-cribed in Project 8 can be used, whereby the two frames are joined together using nails embedded at an angle. This will not be possible if the frame is too thin at the sides, as the nails could easily go right through the side of the frame. An alternative would be to use some kind of clip that can be screwed on, the reverse idea of the spring clip, for instance, to join picture to frame. If the back of the picture extends beyond the frame, an overall paper backing would make a neater finish than gummed paper strips.

When the frame is to hang as a 'diamond' rather than a rectangle it must hang perfectly straight, so take the exact measurements for the screw eyes by measuring down from the top-most corner on each side. The eyes and the wire can then be attached.

Project 10
Restoring an Oil Painting and its Frame

The cleaning and restoration of valuable paintings, drawings and other works of art should be undertaken only by trained conservators. There are some simple types of cleaning and repairing, however, which can be done by an amateur, provided that great care is taken and the art work is not in a critical state of disintegration. An old, dirty and damaged oil painting can be greatly improved by being surface-cleaned, renovated and rewaxed. If it has an old, discoloured and not too badly broken frame this also can be refurbished. Never forget that restoration always demands extreme caution, patience and concentration.

The portrait illustrated here, about 150 years old, is a treasured family keepsake which had remained in the attic as it was in too poor a state to hang. An oil on a fairly thin and brittle canvas, it has several small tears and one or two holes. The varnish has darkened with age, so that some of the details of clothing are obscured. The gilt frame is very grimy, small slivers of the thin plaster on the straight edges have chipped away from the wooden base, and two of the plaster rosette decorations have broken away from their corners. The stretcher is in fairly good condition, but some of the tacks are rusty or have worked loose and need to be replaced.

When a canvas has been on the same stretcher for a long time, dust and debris will accumulate between the canvas and the stretcher on the inside. This is particularly noticeable along the bottom where there may be lumps and bumps showing through. These bulges in the canvas could, in time, cause the paint layer to crack. Although small amounts of dirt can be carefully levered out with a blunt spatula or palette knife, the safest and best way is to take the canvas off the stretcher. It is then possible to check the condition of the stretcher at the same time.

Take great care when embarking on such a task, especially if the canvas is old. The unprimed parts where the canvas is joined to the stretcher will be fragile, and the material may be rotten and tear easily when the tacks are pulled out, especially if the tacks are deeply embedded in the soft wood of the stretcher. If the canvas is too dilapidated to be re-attached to the stretcher satisfactorily, strips of similar canvas can be sewn along the edges as reinforcement. The material must be the same tension as the old canvas or the whole painting will not fit back onto the stretcher neatly.

After the canvas is removed from the stretcher, it should be laid aside carefully, and the stretcher

Left: A very old family portrait, oil on canvas, in the original solid frame with gilt finish. The surface of the painting has a layer of brown grime on the varnish and there is one small tear in the canvas. Strong ripples at each corner of the canvas indicate that it was originally badly stretched, perhaps 'keyed out' too much. The back of the canvas is very dusty and the frame has a coat of surface dirt, chipped edges, and three of the corner rosette decorations are missing, and will need to be replaced.

wiped to remove dust. If there are signs of wood-worm flight holes or wood shavings treat the stretcher with a suitable insecticide in the same way as when treating frames (see page 56). However, if the stretcher is in a generally poor condition – warped or rough so that it may damage the canvas – it will be best to renew it completely. Exact measurements for a new stretcher are essential, as the old stretcher may have been 'keyed' out, with wedges hammered in at the corners which will have stretched it beyond its original size. Therefore measure the canvas across both sides between the start of its 'fold' on the outer edge. The new stretcher should have rounded edges where the canvas will fold over them, so sharp edges must be sanded down.

An oil painting on canvas attached to a stretcher need not be removed from the stretcher for surface cleaning, but should have support underneath as described in Step 2. The transitional area between stretcher piece and open centre of the painting is particularly vulnerable. Use a flat piece of board as a support for the central area, and take care when cleaning over the part which bridges this gap.

Before beginning the surface cleaning using liquids, first carry out a dry cleaning operation. As with paper-based work, the surface dust and fluff should be removed, but not by rubbing. It can be dislodged by lightly brushing with a soft hair brush.

Soap or detergent and water should not be used on oil paintings, as it will soak through a thin paint layer and even through the canvas. I have seen the unfortunate results from well-meaning people who have enthusiastically set about cleaning oil paintings with household scouring powder: because the paint was fairly thick they probably thought that it would not harm either the paint film or penetrate to the canvas or board underneath. However, it is difficult to see the action while it is in progress because the powder is opaque, and a paint layer generally varies in thickness. The result was that interesting brushmark textures were flattened, and the thinner areas were left threadbare with canvas or board showing through as blank patches.

Surface cleaning an oil painting which is only slightly dirty, without removing the varnish, can be done with pure turpentine which is suitable for oil-based work because of its high evaporation rate. If it is applied carefully and allowed to sit for a while, the turpentine will soften the dirt, after which a second application will remove the remaining grime. To remove a more solid layer of dirt, turpentine used in conjunction with a picture cleaner from a reputable artists' suppliers will be necessary. This type of cleaner is a non-acid emulsion of natural resin and essential oils which is specially designed for cleaning varnished oil paintings safely without actually penetrating the varnish. The cleaner softens the dirt so that it can be wiped away with the turpentine which also acts as a neutralizer.

For cleaning, use a good quality surgical cotton wool (cotton), as delicate paint surfaces may be damaged by the fibres of coarser material which can tear at loose or flaking areas of paint film. The action

Step 1

The canvas attached to the stretcher is taken from the old frame. Hold it upright with the bottom resting on a table. Remove old tacks by gripping the head of each tack with pincers and drawing them out carefully to avoid damaging the canvas. If the tacks are rusty or embedded to an extent that makes removal awkward, you can ease them out by using a lever such as a chisel. Take care, however, as stretcher wood is soft and an old canvas may be brittle.

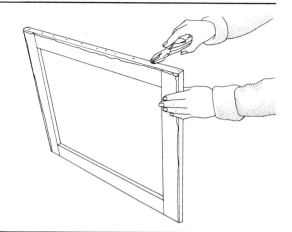

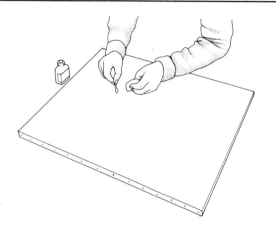

Step 2

Before cleaning the oil, place it on a board support to avoid bending the canvas which may cause the paint surface to crack. Dip little pieces of cotton wool into pure turpentine and clean small areas at a time, using a circular motion and replacing the cotton wool as it becomes dirty. Hold another piece with the other hand and wipe each area as it is cleaned. Use cotton buds or a thin bristle brush to work on small details and places where the surface is irregular, such as areas between the ridges formed by brush strokes.

Step 3

Lay the canvas face down on a piece of glass with waxed tissue paper or blotting paper under the damaged areas. Spread a little adhesive mixture on the canvas around the tear, not too close to the torn edges. Now spread adhesive evenly over one side of the chamfered patch and lay it carefully over the tear, matching the lines of the grain. Press it into position lightly, then lay a piece of waxed paper and glass over it with a weight on top.

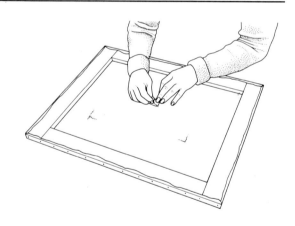

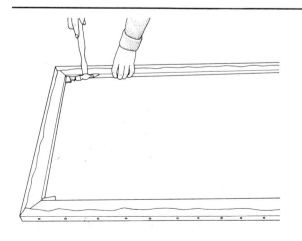

Step 4

After the canvas is re-attached to the stretcher remove any slack in the fabric by keying out the corners with wedges. Replace any missing wedges: there should be two in each corner. Insert them into the cracks of the stretcher and tap each one home gently with a hammer, taking care not to bang too hard as old canvas is delicate and inflexible. The wooden grain of the wedges should run at an angle to the line of the stretcher as there is then less possibility of them falling out.

Step 5

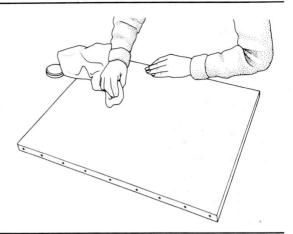

Place a firm support such as a flat board under the stretched canvas and apply beeswax with a soft lint-free cloth. The wax should be warm enough to spread evenly, using a circular motion. Cover the whole painting to the outer edges. Allow the wax to dry thoroughly at normal room temperature before polishing the surface lightly with a clean, soft cloth.

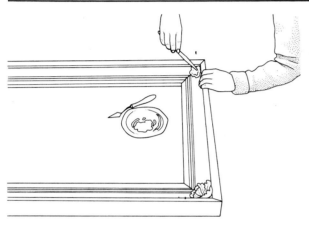

Step 6

If parts of the frame are missing, particularly ornate decorations, these can be rebuilt. Hammer small sharp nails into the broken frame at several points, taking care that the tops of the nails will not extend above the finished ornament. These will act as support for the filler. Build the plaster mixture around the nails, pressing it firmly into place, roughly to the shape and design of the finished piece. If the section is thick, it will be necessary to put on the filler layer by layer, letting each dry out before applying the next. When it has dried out completely you can carve the pattern to match the rest of the frame, using a sharp wood-worker's gouge.

Step 7

Thin cracks and chipped edges on the flat parts of the frame can be filled with barbola paste, shaped and smoothed in one operation. Take a little paste, rub it into a small coil according to the shape and size of the part to be filled, then apply it to the broken area. Press it into shape and smooth away the excess. It will dry fairly quickly and can be sanded lightly before retouching. This paste is also useful for small missing portions of larger ornaments, as it can be shaped easily during application and therefore needs little carving afterwards.

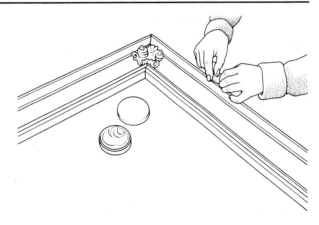

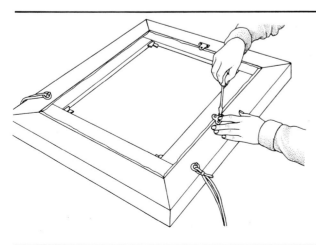

Step 8

Put the frame face down on the table and fit the painting into it. Place a glass plate in the centre of each side so that it bridges the back of both frame and stretcher. Punch through the hole-pieces in the plates into the frame on one side and the stretcher on the other, then insert small screws thus securing the stretcher to the frame. Fitting a picture in this way will avoid jarring a fragile painting with a hammering action, and the picture can be removed easily by simply unscrewing the plates.

should be 'stroking' rather than rubbing. Smaller areas which are difficult to reach are best dealt with by cotton buds as shown in Step 2. There are often tiny obstinate bits such as fly spots or other lumps of congealed dirt, but the surrounding area may be relatively clean, and a larger swab of cotton wool will be clumsy to work with.

During cleaning the painting must not be saturated, but worked over in small areas at a time, and the cotton wool observed constantly for signs of paint colour which may appear if the varnish is thin in parts. An initial cleaning will generally soften the dirt film gradually, but a further cleaning may be necessary. If you look at the edge of the painting that has been hidden under the rebate (rabbet) of the frame, you may see a considerable contrast between colours. The original fresh colours of the painting will be indicated on the edges. It may not be possible to achieve these colours with a mere surface-clean, and professional help is then needed if the painting warrants it.

Bear in mind that tiny crevices or cracks holding dirt will be very difficult to clean and these will be more noticeable as cracking and crazing effects when the surrounding areas are cleaned up. The small hollows caused by the texture of brush strokes may also contain deposits of dirt, and if these are not removed the painting will have an unpleasant mottled colour. A small, thin bristle brush is useful for working on such details as well as the cotton buds.

Extensive damage to oil paintings such as cracking and blistering should be restored by a professional. An invisible repair to a tear or hole will obviously need the standard of retouching which is beyond the amateur. A small tear, however, can be mended at home, by fixing a patch to the back of the canvas as described in Step 3. The patch material should be as close in quality and thickness to the original as possible. Linen is the most suitable fabric as others may not have the same stretching properties and may shrink. One very old repair which I saw done with a piece of card, was buckled and uneven, mainly because it had not been flattened under a heavy weight.

Very old canvases which need to be patched should never be knocked or bent as they are often brittle and thin. A new canvas is generally in a stronger state and quite flexible, so it is easier to match the material for the patch. Sometimes there is sufficient excess around the edges overlapping the stretcher to enable a piece large enough for the patch to be cut away. It is not wise to do this with old canvas, however, as the material is less clean and may be rotten.

To prepare for patching, first clean the area around the tear on the back of the canvas with a soft brush. This will remove any dust that would otherwise prevent the patch from sticking firmly. The patch is cut slightly larger than the damaged area, and its edges 'chamfered' or made thinner and graded by pulling out cross-threads on all four sides. The fringe so formed must be straight when the weight is applied after gluing. Any broken threads on the tear

of the painting should also be cut away. Otherwise, the pressure of weights during the drying and flattening process may cause the edge of the patch to be conspicuous from the front of the canvas as a 'ridge', especially if the canvas and the paint are thin.

Glue is applied around the tear and to the back of the patch, being careful not to disarrange the fringed loose edges. Modern acrylic resins have replaced many of the old glues for both convenience and flexibility. A PVA adhesive, or a wax resin (made by melting three parts of beeswax with two parts of dammar resin and applied while warm) can be used to patch a canvas. If a PVA adhesive is used, it should be allowed to become tacky before joining the two surfaces.

After enough time has elapsed for the patch to dry completely – normally an hour or so – the weights can be lifted away from the canvas. Any excess glue on the front of the painting will have dried to a shiny transparency and it can be cut away very carefully with a sharp blade.

If the tear is an old one, there may be a gap in the fracture or hole whose edges are rough so that they do not meet neatly, and this can be filled in and retouched as necessary. A good paste filler is made from a mixture of whiting powder and PVA adhesive with a little zinc white to act as a preservative. (These can be obtained from hardware or do-it-yourself stores.) A tiny bit of beeswax will help to make a workable consistency. The filler, applied with a small spatula or palette knife, should not overlap the undamaged surrounding areas as the filled area must be the same level as the rest of the painting. If necessary, the filling can be sanded with very fine emerypaper (sandpaper) after it has dried, especially if the texture to be matched is flat.

If it is desirable to simulate the texture of the underlying canvas, a small piece of the same type of canvas can be lightly pressed over the filling, which must not be too liquid or it will lift. Though not easy to do, this produces a satisfying result. It is important to apply the piece so that the grain impression is compatible with the canvas of the painting, and running straight.

To match the right tone of the colour, the patch can be retouched either with acrylic paint which dries quickly or with oil paint mixed with a little retouching varnish which dries more slowly. Such retouching is known as 'in-painting', which implies that the retouching should not extend beyond the damaged area. The extent of restoration is a

Right: The old portrait has been cleaned, patched and waxed, and the frame restored. Note that it is not possible to remove the broad ripples in the brittle canvas without a thorough re-lining done by an expert restorer. The flesh tones of the painting are lighter and small details of the head-dress stand out more clearly. The frame is cleaned, smudges on the gilt removed, missing chips filled and retouched. Missing rosettes have been moulded into each corner and retouched, after which the whole frame has been re-sealed with french polish.

controversial subject in professional circles, but the aim here is to make the painting visually pleasant by covering up a tear or hole which would be distracting. There are numerous methods of imitating the techniques of the painting: brush marks can be simulated by thickened colour; cracking and crazing by using two colours, a darker thread-like network applied to a lighter ground-paint.

After cleaning, the painting can be waxed or re-varnished. The various types of varnish are explained on page 61. A soft wax finish is often preferred to the more shiny one of varnish. (Wax can be applied over varnish but not vice versa.) Beeswax used over varnish reduces the shine and also the risk of 'bloom' or opaque, frosty patches. It may, however, slightly reduce clarity of details, although it is colourless. Mix the wax with turpentine as described in Project 1, and apply carefully. It may be necessary to remove any threads which adhere to the surface with a pair of tweezers before the wax dries. Another advantage of wax is that it can be dissolved and removed easily at a later date by a surface-cleaning.

An old frame being refurbished should first be dusted down and any remaining grime removed with white spirit (turpentine substitute), using wads of cotton wool. Ingrained dirt will be gradually softened, and you may have to work around the frame two or three times. All flaking parts should be removed. It may be necessary to use a stiff bristle brush on ornate areas. Never use ordinary household abrasive cleaners on gilded frames as gold leaf is very thin and will be scratched by harsh cleaning. A damp rag dipped into water which has a drop or two of ammonia added to it will usually remove obstinate particles of dirt.

After the preparatory cleaning has dried, any old pieces or any that have been dislodged during cleaning can be glued back into position. A good way to seal a frame which has an overall tendency to crumble or crack (sometimes the case with ornate design on a plaster base) is to mix a PVA adhesive with a little water to a workable consistency and saturate the frame with it. Use a fairly large brush, forcing the mixture into all the crevices and recesses so that it penetrates thoroughly. The excess glue can be wiped off with a damp rag. This will stop more pieces from breaking off in the future, as it is difficult to tell which parts are loose and a sudden jar can dislodge them.

The cracks which hold the glue will have a semi-transparent, milky colour which can be touched up. If the frame is a muted gold with an over-paint rubbed into the recessed areas between the raised decoration, use a mixture of similar coloured acrylic paint for retouching, and the addition of a little ground pumice powder will give an older look.

Wood filler is useful for covering small cracks, and barbola paste is most suitable for finer missing portions such as chipped edges, and for tiny pieces of filigree or leaf decoration. Larger or wider cracks and holes will need PVA adhesive added to the wood filler to act as a binding agent. If a large chunk of frame or its ornament is missing, a mixture of whiting (very fine plaster) and PVA adhesive blended together with a spatula to a firm but workable consistency can be used for the repair. It is applied as in Step 6, built around nails (using the same principle as building up in sculpture where strong wire forms the base around which to model plaster). The new section should be larger than the surrounding area or intended shape of the piece, so that it can be carved to the exact shape after drying. Flat areas should be sanded to a continuous surface which will be less obvious as a repair.

Once they are thoroughly dried, filled areas should be sealed before they are repainted, as plaster mixtures are porous. The aim of retouching damaged frames is to conceal the repaired area as far as possible, so examine the frame carefully before deciding on the appropriate type and colour of paint. Brightly gilded gold or silver frames should be retouched with patches of gold or silver leaf, as the equivalent paint will appear as dull blotchy areas against such a shiny finish. The old gilt frame of our portrait has a patina of age, and while gold leaf would stand out as too bright a contrast, a slight 'antiquing' or paint rubbed into the gold gives an overall duller finish, so gold wax paste is more appropriate. Here, the gold obviously has a base colour of dull reddish-brown, and so umber mixed with a little red, such as cadmium, is applied first. After the gold paint has dried, a little dark umber is rubbed on. Match the surface texture of the frame by stippling, brushing or dabbing the paint on with a cloth to keep the old rather 'worn' look of the frame.

The ornate corner pieces are first painted with gold wax of a matching shade and allowed to dry, after which the acrylic colour (umber, in this case) is brushed well into the crevices and the residue wiped away from the prominent parts of the cluster pattern, perhaps leaving a smear of colour if the surface of the frame is mottled or uneven. It is harder to conceal repairs on the flat sections of the frame and achieve a perfectly smooth surface of exactly the same colour.

The sides of an old gilt frame are not so noticeable from the front and are usually given a coat of colour which will tone with the gold, a mixture of yellow ochre and dark umber. It is better to paint the entire sides rather than try to touch up small areas, as it is very difficult to match the colour exactly. The whole frame, front and sides, can then be sealed with a coat of clear lacquer for protection.

After fitting the painting back into the frame as described in Step 8, a piece of light card can be attached to the back with drawing-pins. This will prevent dust and debris, as mentioned previously, from collecting between the stretcher and the canvas. The hanging rings, if still on the old frame, should be checked for firmness and strength and replaced if necessary.

Glossary

Acrylic Synthetic resin shaped by a combination of heat and pressure, used as a binding agent in the manufacture of quick-drying acrylic emulsion paint.

Adhesives Made from four sources: plant gums such as Gum Arabic; animal glues such as rabbit-skin, gelatine; vegetable glues for starch pastes such as wheat or rice; synthetic resins such as polyvinyl acetate (PVA).

Antiquing Making the surface of a frame look old by artificial methods using paint, stain or varnish and a stippling, spattering or brushing technique to apply it unevenly, or using a commercial antiquing paste.

Baguette Simple frame structure consisting of four strips of wood, without mitred corners, which are nailed directly onto the picture (usually a stretched canvas).

Barbola paste Fine, smooth modelling paste, easy to manipulate, very useful as a filler for repairing fine details of plaster decorations on old frames.

Bevel Sloping angle at which the inner edge of a mount is cut, depending on the angle at which the knife is held.

Bleaching Cleaning paper-work to remove stains, spots and mildew by submerging it in a solution of chemicals diluted in water.

Bloom Opaque, cloudy patches which sometimes appear on oil paintings after they have been varnished, caused by moisture trapped in the varnish during either application or drying time.

Bole A red clay used as a form of priming before water-gilding on a gesso ground, to provide a suitable surface for burnishing.

Burnishing Rubbing the surface of gold or metal leaf with a hard stone such as agate to obtain a brilliant finish.

Chinagraph pencil Specially prepared for marking polished surfaces such as china or glass.

Conservation (museum) board Acid-free card made entirely of rag, used by reputable museums and galleries for mounting and backing valuable pictures.

Dry mounting Bonding and sealing paper-work or photography under heat and pressure, using thermoplastic tissue.

Fillets Strips of wood used in a frame combination such as shadow box to provide space between the framed object and the glass; a thin 'under' mount (mat) of a contrasting colour added to the main mount.

Fitch brush Small, flat bristle brush sloping to a point, used for lining and painting narrow channels on frames.

Foxing Small brown spots on older types of paper, especially that made from wood pulp. They are caused by acid migration and will increase with time unless the action is arrested by bleaching.

Gesso Fine, powdered plaster of Paris mixed with water and rabbit-skin glue, which provides a solid smooth base for painting and gilding. Acrylic gesso is made of synthetic resin in place of the animal glue, and is also available from art stores.

Gilder's tip Broad, flat soft-hair brush used for picking up and transferring gold or metal leaf to the surface to be gilded.

Gilding The process of applying thin sheets of pounded metal to the surface of a frame which has a base of gesso, and a thin coating of either oil- or water-based adhesive.

Grain The direction or texture of wood or fabric formed by lines running in the same direction.

Lining pen A pen with two sides of the nib joined with a small screw. The width of the line can be adjusted by manipulating the screw.

Mitre box A metal or wooden framing tool into which moulding is clamped and cut at a perfect angle with a tenon saw. Normal frames have a 45° angle, but it is possible to adjust a metal box to cut other angles when making other than four-sided frames.

Moulding Wood in a variety of shapes bought by the length for cutting and joining to make a frame. Picture frame moulding has a rebated (cut away) section which fits over the edge of the picture. Moulding from general wood merchants does not have this, and needs an extra piece of wood joined to the reverse to supply a rebate (rabbet).

Mount (mat) A surround with a window opening for the picture, usually of a thick card base, but can be covered in a variety of coloured and textured papers and fabrics. It keeps the picture flat and prevents it from direct contact with the glass and provides a visually pleasing space between the picture and its frame.

Ornament and decoration on moulding

Cushion A moulding, convex in section, usually bordered either side with a narrow beading. Often used to describe the curved surface of a frame.

Egg-and-dart A convex running pattern of alternating egg shapes and points or leaves, derived from Greek decorative mouldings. Generally the perimeter moulding on classical picture frames.

Gadrooning An enrichment consisting of flutes or convex reeds in a repeating pattern, often centred, running out to corners.

Guilloche Continuous interlaced curving bands like twisted ribbons, used to enrich mouldings or flat surfaces.

Leaf-and-tongue A variant of egg-and-dart (see above) in which the oval is replaced by leaf forms. Usually occurs on the inner edge of the frame which touches the painting.

Ogee An 'S' shaped moulding that consists of a double curve, the outer concave, the inner convex. It forms the basic profile of many eighteenth-century frame designs.

Ribbon-and-stick A pattern in the form of a ribbon or rod.

Strapwork Intricate patterns of interlaced lines and scrolls, interspersed with geometrical figures, probably originated in Antwerp early in the sixteenth century.

Passe-partout tape A plastic or cloth adhesive tape in a variety of colours used to join glass to backing board around the edges, with the picture sandwiched between.

Patina The naturally antique surface on wood or metal objects or frames which has developed over a long period of time or through much use.

Perspex (Plexiglass etc) Transparent acrylic sheets often used as a substitute for glass in framing. Although lightweight and unbreakable, it tends to scratch easily if handled carelessly.

Plate-mark In etchings, engravings, etc., the impression left by the edges of the wooden or metal plate when the paper is stamped in the printing press.

Polystyrene foam (Styrofoam) Synthetic thermoplastic material, usually white, available in sheet form or small squares in various thicknesses, and often used in packing and interior decoration to line wall surfaces.

Rebate (rabbet) The cut-away section on the inner side of a piece of moulding in which the glass, picture and backing fit.

Rebate size The exact measurement of the rebate on a frame and it is slightly larger than the actual picture size. The sight size is the exact measurement of the inner edge of the frame.

Resins Natural resin is the gummy sap obtained from trees and plants and the various types (eg dammar, copal and mastic) are used in the preparation of protective varnishes for oil paintings. Synthetic resins are becoming more popular in varnishes because of their greater flexibility and less likelihood of turning brown with age.

Size A glutinous substance applied to paper, gesso etc. to provide a suitable surface for painting, gilding etc.

Slip (liner) An inner frame with a wooden base, covered in fabric or gilded, which serves as a transitional section between frame and picture in the same way as a mount, and is usually used on an oil or acrylic painting.

Stretcher A framework of interlocking wooden bars to which a canvas is attached with tacks. Two wedges are tapped lightly into the slots at each corner to 'key out' the canvas until it becomes taut.

Styrofoam (see Polystyrene)

Thermoplastics Synthetic materials (acrylic sheets) that melt under heat and harden when cooled.

Varnish Protective coating with resin or synthetic base applied to wood or oil paintings to provide a glossy finish.

Wet mounting Laying paper-work onto a backing of card or board, first damping the paper and then applying the adhesive. The paper is then joined to the backing and flattened by hand or with a roller.

Wood stains The three types are: oil, (colour pigment mixed with oil such as turpentine or white spirit); spirit, (pigment mixed with alcohol or methylated spirits); water, (usually dyes mixed with water and sometimes more vivid than the normal earth colours).

Further Reading

ALLEN, J. *Studio Vista Guide to Craft Suppliers* (Studio Vista, London 1974)

BURNETT, L. and R. *The Picture Framer's Handbook* (Clarkson N. Potter, New York 1973; Hodder & Stoughton, London 1973)

BURNS, J. T. *Framing Pictures* (Herbert Press, London 1978)

CHAMBERS, D. L. *How to Gold Leaf Antiques and Other Objects* (Allen & Unwin, London 1973)

DOERNER, M. *The Materials of the Artist* (Granada Publishing, London 1979)

DUREN, L. *Frame It* (Houghton Mifflin, New York 1976)

FOURACRE, J. *Picture Framing* (Search Press, London 1973)

GARRARD, P. J. (Ed) *The Artist's Guide* (Billboard Publications – Cardfont, London 1976)

GETTENS, R. J. and G. L. STOUT *Painting Materials: A Short Encyclopaedia* (Dover, New York 1966)

GRIMM, G. *Alte Bilderrahmen* (Georg D. W. Callwey, Munich 1978)

HAYES, C. *The Complete Guide to Painting and Drawing Techniques and Materials* (Phaidon, Oxford 1979)

HEYDENRYK, H. *The Art and History of Picture Frames* James H. Heinemann, Inc, New York 1963)

KAY, R. *The Painter's Guide to Studio Methods and Materials* (Studio Vista, London 1973; Doubleday, New York 1973)

KELLY, F. *Art Restoration* (David & Charles, Newton Abbott 1971)

MASSEY, R. *Formulas for Artists* (Batsford, London 1968)

MAYER, R. *The Artist's Handbook of Materials and Techniques* (Faber & Faber, London 1978)

MILLS, J. F. *Picture Cleaning and Restoration* (Winsor & Newton, London)

NEWMAN, T. J. & L. *The Frame Book* (Crown, New York 1974)

NUTTALL, P. *Picture Framing for Beginners* (Studio Vista, London 1970; Watson Guptill, New York 1970)

RUHEMANN, H. *The Cleaning of Paintings: Problems and Potentialities* (Faber & Faber, London 1968; Praeger, New York 1968)

TOSCANO, E. *Framing* (Pan Books, London 1974)

WOODS, M. *Mounting and Framing Pictures* (Batsford, London 1978)

WOOLLARD, L. *Picture Framing* (John Gifford, London 1970)

Acknowledgments and Photo-Credits

The author and publishers are extremely grateful to the following people who kindly loaned their pictures or objects to be framed or photographed on pages: 116 and 121 Mrs Gunvor Avery; 64 and 70 Miss Marie-Louise Avery; 84 and 90/1 Mr Antonio Barreiros; 34/5, 50 Mr Karl Barrie of The Kaleidoscope Gallery, 66 Willesden Lane, London NW6; 42, 43, 47 top and bottom, 78 and 83 Mr and Mrs Alan Edwards, 18 Abbotstone Road, London SW15; 104 and 109 Mr Werner Forman; 55 Mr Peter Kibbles; 110 and 116 Mrs Vera Haslam; 56 and 63, 92 and 96/7 Miss Tristram Holland; 53 Miss Suzanne Lodge; 44/5 Cowling & Wilcox, Art Suppliers, 26 Broadwick Street, London W1; 46 (artist's proof of *Le Mont St Michel*) Mrs Marshall Stewart; 98 and 103 Mr Michael Raeburn; 2/3 and 32/3, 2, 26/7, 37, 40, 48/9 Mr

Jonathan Savill of The Rowley Gallery, 115 Kensington Church Street, London W1; 1 Mrs C. F. W. Salmon; 10, 23 Mr Richard Salmon; 8, 11, 30, 38, 39 Mr and Mrs G. Wansell.

The publishers are also grateful to Coral Mula for her work on the line drawings and to the following for permission to reproduce the photographs on pages: 22 Detroit Institute of Arts (Georges Seurat, *View of Crotoy, Amont*, 1889, oil on canvas, bequest of Robert H. Tannahill 70.183); 23 Mr Eduardo Paolozzi; 1 Mr Patrick Procktor; 18 Musée du Louvre, Paris; 20 National Trust, London; 17 Rijksmuseum, Amsterdam; 12 Scala, Florence; 21 Trustees of the National Gallery, London.

Index

Guide to Materials and Suppliers in the UK

Tools, paints, wood stains, board, glass and other sundries can be obtained from local hardware shops, do-it-yourself stores and glaziers, which are listed in any local telephone directory. Materials such as acrylic paints, paper, card and fine brushes are available at general artists' suppliers throughout the country. Other useful sources can be found in the classified sections of art and craft magazines. The following is a brief list of stores which carry special items.

BLOCK MOUNTING/HEAT-SEALING
Kay's Mounting Service, 351 Caledonian Road, London N1.

GENERAL ART MATERIALS
Allenton Homecrafts, 859 Osmaston Road, Allenton, Derby, Derbyshire.
Arts and Handicrafts, 18 Station Parade, Harrogate, Yorkshire.
The Arts and Craft Shop, 194 Union Street, Oldham, Lancashire.
Arts and Crafts, 241 Greasby Road, Wirral, Cheshire.
Baker Street Art Shop, 54 Baker Street, London W1.
Brodie & Middleton Ltd, 79 Long Acre, London WC2.
Cowling & Wilcox Ltd, 26 Broadwick Street, London W1.
Dolphin Crafts, Dolphin House, Mill Street, Chagford, Devon.
Green & Stone Ltd, 259 King's Road, London SW3.
Handicrafts (Peterborough), New Road, Peterborough, Huntingdonshire.
Langford & Hill Ltd, Graphic House, 10 Warwick Street, London W1.
Morrison's Artists' Materials, Nithsdale Road Post Office, Glasgow.
Reeves & Co Ltd, 178 Kensington High Street, London W8.
Rowney & Co Ltd, 12 Percy Street, London W1.
Winsor & Newton Ltd, 51-2 Rathbone Place, London W1.

GILDING MATERIALS/LEAF/POWDER
E. Ploton Ltd, 273 Archway Road, London N6.
George Whiley Ltd, The Runway, Station Approach, South Ruislip, Middlesex.

GLASS/PERSPEX/MIRRORS
R. Denny & Co Ltd, 13 Netherwood Road, London W14.

HAND-MADE PAPER/MOUNT CARD
Barcham Green, Hayle Mill, Maidstone, Kent.
R. K. Burt & Co, 37 Union Street, London SE1.
Falkiner Fine Papers, 4 Mart Street, London WC2.
Lawrence & Aitken Ltd, Albion Works, Kimberley Road, London NW6.
Midland Educational Co Ltd, 104/106 Corporation Street, Birmingham, Warwickshire.
Paperchase, 215 Tottenham Court Road, London, W1.

IRONMONGERY/HANGING FIXTURES/TOOLS/SUNDRIES
Beardmore & Co Ltd, 5 Percy Street, London W1.
Buck & Ryan Ltd, 101 Tottenham Court Road, London W1.
Burgess & Galer Ltd, 51 Brewer Street, London W1.
W. Pond & Co Ltd, 192-194 Corporation Street, Birmingham, Warwickshire.
F. B. Scragg & Co, 68 Victoria Street, Birmingham.
Sefco Ltd (Shortwood Carvings), 6-9 Timber Street, London EC1.
Shiner & Sons Ltd, Windmill Street, London W1.

LINEN/CANVAS FABRICS
Kantex Ltd, 22 Rathbone Place, London W1.
Russell & Chapple Ltd, 23 Monmouth Street, London WC2.

MACHINE-MADE PAPER
Inveresk Paper Co Ltd, 19 Tudor Street, London EC4.
Wiggins Teape, Gateway House, Basing View, Basingstoke, Hampshire.

METAL & PLASTIC FRAME KITS
The Compleat Artist, 102 Crane Street, Salisbury, Wiltshire.
Cowling & Wilcox Ltd, 26 Broadwick Street, London W1.
Daler Board Co Ltd, Wareham, Dorset.
Hang-It Ltd, 225 Greenwich High Road, London SE10.
Johae Art Centre, 17 St John's Street, Colchester, Essex.
Picturewise Ltd, 11 Tottenham Mews, London W1.

PICTURE FRAME MOULDINGS/WOODS
J. Fisher & Son, 21 Bevenden Street, London N1.
General Woodwork Supplies, 76-80 Stoke Newington High Street, London N16.
The Handicraft Shop, Central Station Buildings, Queen Street, Exeter, Devon.
Rosenstiel's, 33 Marham Street, Chelsea Green, London SW3.
Scharf Mouldings, 145 Stoke Newington High Street, London N16.

PIGMENTS/RESINS/WAXES
L. Cornelissen & Son, 22 Great Queen Street, London WC2.

WOOD STAINS/POLISHES
Rustins Ltd, Drayton Works, Waterloo Road, London NW2.

WOODWORM TREATMENT
Rentokil Ltd, 16 Dover Street, London W1.